JOSHUA

AND THE LAND OF PROMISE

JOSHUA

AND THE LAND OF PROMISE

By

F. B. Meyer, B.A.

CHRISTIAN • LITERATURE • CRUSADE
Fort Washington, Pennsylvania 19034

CHRISTIAN LITERATURE CRUSADE

U.S.A.
Box 1449, Fort Washington, PA 19034

GREAT BRITAIN
51 The Dean, Alresford, Hants., SO24 9BJ

AUSTRALIA
P.O. Box 91, Pennant Hills, N.S.W. 2120

NEW ZEALAND
P.O. Box 1203 Palmerston North

Originally published by Fleming H. Revell Co.

Published in the United Kingdom by
Marshall, Morgan & Scott Ltd.

First American edition 1977
Reprinted 1993

ISBN 87508-357-9

Cover Picture: SuperStock Inc.

Printed in the United States of America

PREFACE

THE best way to vindicate the Bible is to preach it. Each book contains within itself, sometimes in hidden form, the autograph of the Holy Spirit. Every page has the watermark of Heaven. And a patient consideration of the contents of Scripture, as of the book before us, will leave a stronger impression of God's authority and authorship than any number of external evidences.

In addition to this, and altogether apart from the spiritual lessons that may be derived from a devout study of Old Testament Scriptures, there accrues to the thoughtful mind an ever-deepening conviction that, instrumentally, they date from the pens of contemporary historians. It is impossible to believe that a writer sometime after the return from exile could have told the story of Joshua with the vividness, the realism, the minute lifelike touches, in which it is presented to us in the historical books of the Old Testament. In the perspective of time, many things that bulk largely to their contemporaries are dismissed as unworthy of notice, while general principles are discussed to the ignoring of details. But the reverse of these meets us in every paragraph of that wonderful series of books of which the story of Joshua is one.

This study, in which the scenes of the conquest of Canaan are narrated again with such help as modern investigation affords, may thus confirm the wavering faith of some. But my main object has been to bring out the wonderful parallels between the story of this book and the experiences of the Church and the individual Christian—parallels so minute and precise as to establish with added force our faith in the Bible as one book, the production of one mind, which "at sundry times and in diverse manners" has spoken to men.

In writing this book I have read, among other works, Dean Stanley's *Jewish Church*; *Joshua, His Life and Times*, by Rev. W. J. Deane; *The Book of Joshua*, by H. F. Witherby; *The Fullness of Blessing*, by S. F. Smiley; and other smaller books—to all of which I gladly confess my obligations.

F. B. Meyer

CONTENTS

1

THE BOOK OF JOSHUA

"What if Earth
Be but the shadow of Heaven—and things therein
Each to other like, more than on earth is thought!"
MILTON

THE order of the books of the Old Testament is due to something more than human selection, or even the period of their composition. The same Spirit who originally inspired them has manifestly controlled their position in the sacred Book. Genesis begins with God, and leads us back to the origin of that divine grace which strives against human sin, loves man before there is anything in man to warrant it, and binds itself by a covenant, "ordered in all things and sure." Exodus tells the story of redemption; Leviticus, of worship; Numbers, of our position in the ordered ranks of God's army; Deuteronomy, of that more spiritual conception of the law of God which is produced by love and faith; and the Book of Joshua is an indispensable link in this chain of symbolical teaching. Finally, the history of the soul may be traced through the disorder of Judges to the royalty of the Kings; and onward to the hallelujahs of the Psalms, and the prophetic visions of the following books.

There is, then, a special inner meaning in the Book of Joshua, which cannot be exhausted when we have learned from it the story of the extermination of the Canaanites; of the partition and settlement of Canaan; and of the noble simplicity and military exploits of Joshua. It is impossible to suppose that so much space should have been given to the record of these details unless there had been some deep and holy purpose— similar to that which has given such minute directions for the Levitical sacrifices, each of which contained some deep spiritual truth required for the growth of holy souls throughout the ages. Of the Book of Joshua, as of the Paschal Lamb and the passage of the Red Sea, it may be said, "All these things happened unto them by way of example" (1 Cor. 10:11, R.V.).

The clue to this inner meaning is given by the writer of the Epistle to the Hebrews, the third and fourth chapters of which are all-important in determining the drift of our interpretation; and it is to the clearer appreciation of the true meaning of these chapters that we must attribute the increasing interest with which the Church of God turns to this record of the simple-minded, transparent, humble, and strong soldier—the Miles Standish* of the Exodus. Before we come to the conquest and partition of the land, consider this: if the river Jordan stands for physical death, and Canaan for heaven—as some suppose—there seems to be no satisfactory interpretation for many items which are narrated with significant minuteness; and on this line of interpretation there would be some anomaly in associating fighting with the calm restfulness of the New Jerusalem.

A careful study of the chapters referred to shows us that Canaan is *not* a picture of future rest with God but a vivid type of that blessed Sabbath-keeping into which we may enter here and now. In Hebrews 4:1–11 we are told to fear lest we "should seem to come short" of the rest, even as they whose carcasses fell in the wilderness

---

* Captain of the Pilgrims, who led expeditions against the Indians.

came short of the Land of Promise. "We which have believed *do* enter into that rest." Our Lord Jesus has entered into his rest, as God did into his; he has therefore received the ideal Land of Canaan as the representative of his followers, to whom he allots it as they believe. We are summoned to give diligence to enter into that rest, that "no man fall after the same example of disobedience" (R.V.).

All these references go to establish the spiritual significance of this wonderful story, which tells of that satisfaction of rest, wealth, and victory which may be enjoyed by those who have come to know the secret things which God has prepared for those who love him, and which are revealed by his Spirit. Oh that that Spirit may use these chapters for the purpose of leading many of God's redeemed ones from the wilderness life into that rest! For that we have been redeemed. For that we have passed through the Red Sea. To convince us of our need of that we have been permitted to hunger and thirst in the desert waste. And our possession of that rest will alone convince the world that the Lord Jesus is the Christ of God. We were indeed brought out that we might be brought in; redeemed that we might be sanctified and glorified.

There is a book in the New Testament in deep spiritual accord with the story told in the Book of Joshua, namely, the Epistle to the Ephesians. This book rises above all its kin as the soaring cathedral tower rises above the maze of architecture beneath—on which it rests indeed, but which it crowns, and carries within its heart bells that ring out the wedding peal. Already in that epistle we can detect notes which are to announce the consummation of creation in the marriage of the Lamb. The Book of Joshua is to the Old Testament what the Epistle to the Ephesians is to the New.

The characteristic phrase occurring in Ephesians is *the heavenlies* (1:3, 20; 2:6; 3:10; 6:12). This does not stand for heaven but for that spiritual experience of oneness with the risen Saviour in his resurrection and exaltation which is the privilege of all the saints, to which, indeed, they have been called, and which is theirs in him. It may help us to a better comprehension of this analogy between the "heavenly places" and the land of Canaan if we trace this in the following five particulars:

1. EACH WAS THE DESTINED GOAL TO WHICH GOD'S PURPOSE LED HIS PEOPLE. When in answer to the agony of his people's cry, and in remembrance of his covenant, the Lord appeared to Moses at the burning bush, in the first sentence he spoke he pledged himself not only to deliver his people out of the land of the Egyptians but to bring them up out of that land into a good and spacious land, to a land flowing with milk and honey. Their emancipation from slavery to Pharaoh was only preparatory to their settlement in the Land of Promise.

Some vision of this seems to have shone like a star before the march of the ransomed hosts; and on the shores of the Red Sea their triumphant strains passed from the destruction of their foes to the mountain of God's inheritance, whither he would bring them in and plant them.

> "The place, O Lord, which thou hast
> made for thee to dwell in.
> The sanctuary, O Lord, which thy
> hands have established."

The plagues of Egypt that struck the fetters from the wrists of an enslaved nation, the institution of the Passover and shedding of blood, the passage of the Red Sea and destruction of the hosts of Egypt—all must have been abortive had they not led on to, and been consummated in, the settlement of Israel in Canaan. Nor otherwise could the divine promise to Abraham have been fulfilled—"Lift up now thine eyes, and look from

Go To Highest Place in Durham?

the place where thou art northward, and southward, and eastward, and westward: for all the land which thou seest, to thee will I give it, and to thy seed forever."

Similarly, though so many of the Lord's redeemed ones seem ignorant of it, all the wonderful facts that lie behind the history of the Church were intended to clear the ground, to level the hills and fill up the valleys, so as to prepare for all who believe the glad entrance into the blessed life—into an experience like that which was enjoyed by the Master himself during his earthly ministry: joy that must forever be a song without words, peace that passes understanding, love that passes knowledge.

It is remarkable how constantly the Epistles point to this experience. The foundations of justification are massively and deeply laid, that they may carry the edifice of sanctification and blessedness. The apostles do not write their glowing paragraphs for the conversion of the world, or the awakening of the dead; rather, they write for the perfecting of the saints and the unfolding of the true conditions of holiness, and victory, and power.

Let me here solemnly ask, have you realized those conditions, and entered on those privileges? Are you still in the wilderness, or have you entered the Land of Promise? Do you occupy cities you never built; eat of vineyards and olive-yards you never planted; drink of cisterns filled from the everlasting hills which you have never hewed; and inhabit houses full of all good things which you never stored? Do you dwell in a land of corn and wine, while the heavens drop dew? Do you, as the beloved of the Lord, dwell between his shoulders? Do you tread down your enemies beneath shoes of iron or brass? Do you make your dwelling-place in the eternal God, while underneath are his everlasting arms? Test yourself by the promises made to Israel, which are types and shadows of eternal realities; and if they do not foreshadow facts in your spiritual experience, understand that you frustrate the purpose of God in your redemption. Leave those things which are behind to reach forth to the goodly land beyond the Jordan, taking hold of that for which you were taken hold of by Christ Jesus.

2. EACH WAS IMPOSSIBLE BY THE MEANS OF LAW. "Now after the death of Moses the servant of the Lord, it came to pass that the Lord spake unto Joshua the son of Nun, Moses' minister, saying, Moses my servant is dead; now therefore arise, go over this Jordan." "The law came by Moses," and in a very real sense found in him its representative. So it was befitting that, when he died, his eye should not be dim, nor his natural force abated. The law of God can never become decrepit or show signs of weakness and decay. At the end of uncounted ages it is as strong, and fresh, and vigorous as that divine nature of which it is the expression.

But the law of God can never bring the soul of man into the Land of Promise; not because of any defect in it, but because of human infirmity and sin. In that marvelous piece of self-analysis given us in the Epistle to the Romans, the apostle repeatedly affirms that the law is holy and righteous and good; he insists that he delighted in it after the inward man, but he tells us that he finds another law in his members, warring against the law of his mind and bringing him into captivity. It is the presence of this evil law in our members which makes obedience to the law of God impossible, filling us with disappointment and unrest, ceaseless striving and perpetual failure. We must, therefore, leave the law as an outward rule of life behind us, in that lonely valley over against Bethpeor (Deut. 3:29), so that the divine Joshua may lead us into the Land of Promise.

Not by vows, or resolutions, or covenants of consecration signed by blood fresh drawn from the veins; not by external rites or by ascetic abstinence from good and healthy things; not by days of fasting and nights of prayer; not even by obedience to the voice of conscience

THE Land of BLESSEDNESS
" " " VICTORY
" " " REST
" " " Full ENJOYMENT

or the inner light—though attention to these is of prime importance—shall we enter the land of blessedness. They all become forms of legalism when practiced with a view of obtaining the full rest and victory of Christian experience. Valuable many of them unquestionably are, when the river is crossed and the land is entered; but they will not of themselves unlock its gates, or roll back its guardian river. Just as the forgiveness of sins and eternal life are the free gift of God's grace, to be received by faith—though their full enjoyment is determined by obedience and self-denial—so the fullness of the blessing of the gospel of Christ is bestowed on those only who, in the absence of all merit and effort, receive it with open and empty hands. We do not work up to our rest-day, as the Jews did, but down from it.

3. EACH WAS ENTRUSTED TO A REPRESENTATIVE. It is a remarkable characteristic of the story of Joshua that God repeatedly addresses him for the people, and bestows on him what was destined for them. "Go over this Jordan, thou, and all this people. . . . There shall not any man be able to stand before thee." "See, I have given into thine hand Jericho, and the king thereof." And it was for him to apportion it. "Thou shalt cause this people to inherit the land which I sware unto their fathers to give them." All was put into the hands of Joshua, as the trustee of Israel, for him to administer as each of the tribes came near to appropriate it from his hands.

And in perfect keeping with this we find it stated, at the close of the seven years' war, that "Joshua took the whole land, according to all that the Lord said unto Moses; and Joshua gave it for an inheritance unto Israel according to their divisions by their tribes" (Josh. 11:23).

How perfectly is this type fulfilled in our blessed Lord! To him as the trustee and representative of his people has all spiritual blessing been given, and he holds it for us to claim. All power is given to him in heaven and on

WE ARE UNDER SHEPHERDS

earth, that he might give us authority over all the power of the enemy. The Father has given him to have life in himself, that he might give us life more abundantly. He is full of grace and truth, that out of his fullness we all may receive. He received from the Father the promise of the Holy Spirit, that he might pour him forth in Pentecostal fullness. He has received from the Father honor and glory, that we might be with him where he is. *THEN POURED ON THE BE*

Let us diligently comprehend all the fullness of our inheritance in Jesus; and then let us go forward to apprehend it by faith. Whatever he has is *in trust* for us. Let us claim it! Let us receive the abundance of his grace, that we may reign in this life through the one Man! Let us believe that we receive, and reckon on it, living in the power of what we may not feel but know we have—in *active faith.*

4. EACH WAS MISSED BY MANY. Their carcasses fell in the wilderness, so that the generation who cried, "Would God that we had died in the wilderness!" did in fact die there. The Ninetieth Psalm tells the tale of those sad and dreary years, when an unceasing train of funerals passed out from the camp of Israel, and the mounds of the desert traced the course of the guilty and unbelieving race.

Such scenes are witnessed still. And the state of his Church must be a bitter sorrow to the heart of her Lord. Notwithstanding his agony and bloody sweat, his cross and passion; in spite of the earnest remonstrance of his Word and Spirit; though the fair land of Canaan lies within view—yet so few comparatively appear to have realized what he intended. All around, souls redeemed by his blood, who have been numbered among his people, are perishing outside the land of blessedness in graves of worldliness, of self-indulgence, and masterful sin. We discover here and there a Joshua, a Caleb, or a tribe of Levites, but the majority seem to have fallen short. See to it, reader, that you are not one of them! "Let us also fear."

5. EACH WAS INFESTED BY MANY ADVERSARIES. The seven nations of Canaan held the land with strongholds and chariots of iron—though the Lord caused them to be to his people as bread which needs only to be eaten. They came against the invading hosts in all the pride of their vast battalions and the array of their warlike preparations. But at his rebuke they fled; at the voice of his thunder they hasted away.

The "heavenly places" also are not removed from the noise of conflict, or free from the presence of the foe. Those who are raised to sit there in Christ have to encounter the spiritual hosts of wickedness, principalities and powers of evil. They are conquered foes; but, nevertheless, they are terrible to behold, and certain to overcome—unless we are abiding in our great Joshua, who has already vanquished them, and have taken to ourselves the whole armor of God.

Thus the land of Canaan and the heavenly places are one: and we may read into these ancient records the deepest thoughts of the New Testament, for God repeats himself in many ways.

2

THE DIVINE COMMISSION

(JOSHUA 1:7)

"Only when thine arm
In sense of weakness reaches forth to God,
Wilt thou be strong to suffer and to do."
PLUMPTRE

AS Joshua stood on the threshold of his great work, he was repeatedly bidden to be strong and full of courage. Some little time before the death of his predecessor, a great convocation of all Israel had been summoned, at which Moses had solemnly transferred his office to his successor and had given him a charge, saying, "Be strong and of a good courage; for thou must go with this people unto the land" (Deut. 31:7). And now the voice of God reiterates the charge and repeats the injunction.

At first this startles us. What! Must all they whom God uses be strong? Is it essential that there should be strength of limb and muscle in the physical and moral constitution of those who are called to do the divine biddings in the world? Because, if that be so, we who are like Ehud, left-handed; like Gideon, least in our father's house; or like Saul of Tarsus, painfully conscious of weakness, can never get beyond the rank and file in the army of the Lord.

And yet, may not this reiterated appeal indicate that the heart of Joshua misgave him, and that he was conscious of his utter inadequacy to fulfill the great commission that was thrust upon him? Probably he had never dreamed of so high an honor, so vast a responsibility. He had been content to be Moses' aide, satisfied to wait below while his master passed into the cloud to hold fellowship with God; staying in the tent to serve Moses if he were required, or in his absence to guard its contents; jealous for his master's honor, when Eldad and Medad prophesied; glad that all the glories of the conquest of Eastern Palestine decked with laurels the closing days of the great leader.

When Moses first received the sentence of death on the further side of Jordan, none could have been more deeply grieved than his faithful friend and attendant. But the thought of succeeding him never presented itself to his mind. Indeed, Moses himself does not appear to have thought of him in this direction; for we learn that he besought the Lord to appoint a man over the congregation, that they should not be as sheep without a shepherd (Num. 27:17). In that prayer Joshua may have joined, thinking all the while that Caleb, the lion-hearted, or Phinehas the priest, or one of the sons of Moses, might take his place—but not supposing that he would himself be called to it. His one aim had been to enhance the glory and lighten the cares of Moses, and he was too absorbed in his master's personality to be greatly conscious of his own.

When therefore the call came to him to assume the office which Moses was vacating, his heart failed him, and he needed every kind of encouragement and stimulus, both from God and man. "Be strong" shows that he felt weak; "Be of good courage" shows that he was affrighted; "Be not thou dismayed" shows that he seriously considered whether he would not have to give up the task. He was a worm, and no man: how should he deliver Israel?

It is when men are in this condition that God approaches them with the summons to undertake vast and overwhelming responsibilities. Most of us are too strong for him to use; we are too full of our own schemes and plans and ways of doing things. He must empty us, and humble us, and bring us down to the dust of death, so low that we need every straw of encouragement, every leaf of help; and then he will raise us up, and make us as the rod of his strength. The world talks of the survival of the fittest; but God gives power to the faint, and increases might to them that have no strength; he perfects his strength in weakness, and uses things that are not to bring to naught things that are. If Ehud had been right-handed, he might never have judged Israel; if Gideon had been the greatest instead of the least in his father's house, he would never have vanquished Midian; if Paul had been as eloquent in his speech as he confesses himself to have been contemptible, he would never have preached the gospel from Jerusalem all the way around to Illyricum.

Let us consider the sources of Joshua's strength:

1. A FAITHFUL PAST. "After the death of Moses the servant of the Lord, the Lord spake unto Joshua the son of Nun, Moses' minister." In his case, as always, the eternal rule held good, that faithfulness in a few things is the condition of rule over many things; and the loyalty of a servant is the stepping-stone to the royalty of the throne. Of the Highest it is said that he was obedient to death, even the death of the cross; and that, therefore, God highly exalted him, and gave him the Name above every name. We must learn obedience by the things that we suffer before we can be lifted from the dunghill to sit with princes.

The previous years of Joshua's past had been full of high and noble endeavor. For forty years, if Josephus be correct in his statement as to his age at the death of Moses, he shared the slavery and sorrows of a captive race. His childish eyes must have become accustomed to witnessing the brutality of the Egyptian taskmasters, even if his own shoulders were not torn by their cruel whips. As a scion of one of the leading families of Ephraim (Num. 13:8, 16) he may have taken some leading part in the marshaling of the Exodus, and there approved himself as worthy of all trust. His conflict with Amalek; his good report of the Land of Promise; his refusal to take any part in the disastrous attack on the Canaanites; his eagerness for the good name and fame of Moses; his patient endurance of the weary years of wandering—all prove that his was no common character. The aloe blooms only once in a hundred years; but every hour of all that century is needed to produce the delicate texture and resplendent beauty of the flower. The valiant deed of a Grace Darling* is not the sudden outburst of the moment that gives it birth, but the result of long years of self-discipline, courage, and ministry to others. And this summons of Joshua to the leader's place in Israel was the reward of more than eighty years of faithful service.

None of us can tell for what God is educating us. We fret and murmur at the narrow round and daily task of ordinary life, not realizing that it is only thus that we can be prepared for the high and holy office which awaits us. We must descend before we can ascend. We must suffer if we would reign. We must take the *via crucis* (the way of the cross) submissively and patiently if we would tread the *via lucis* (the way of light). We must endure the polishing if we would be shafts in the quiver of Emmanuel. God's will comes to you and me in daily circumstances, in little things equally as in great. Meet them bravely; be at your best always, though the occasion be one of the very least; dignify the smallest summons

---

* A 19th century English heroine who rescued nine shipwrecked mariners.

by the greatness of your response. So the call will come to you as to Joshua the son of Nun, Moses' aide.

2. A DISTINCT CALL. "Arise, go over this Jordan, thou, and all this people, unto the land which I do give to them. . . . Be strong and of a good courage, for thou shalt cause this people to inherit the land which I sware unto their fathers to give them." When a man knows that he has been called to do a certain work, he is invincible. No, he is not unconscious of his own deficiencies, whether they be natural or intellectual. He is not insensible of difficulty; no one is so quick as he to see the great stones, the iron gates, the walled cities, the broad and flowing rivers. He is not invulnerable to the shafts of ridicule and adverse criticism. Despite all this he looks steadily away to the declared purpose of God, and yields himself to be the channel through which it may operate.

Joshua's task was a very difficult one. The people of Canaan were well versed in the arts and sciences of the time, acquired from commerce with the Phoenicians on the north and the Egyptians on the south. One of the most interesting discoveries of recent years has shown that the Hittites were a great people, highly cultured, and of sufficient importance to rival Assyria and Egypt. It seemed preposterous to suppose that a nation of a few years' existence was so soon to dispossess nations that had gained the country by conquest and were prepared to fight for every inch of territory by the most approved methods of warfare. The Jewish legend says that when Joshua, appalled at the greatness of the task, rent his clothes and fell on his face, weeping to think of his incompetence, Moses lifted him up and comforted him with the assurance that God had foreseen and provided for all. Whether it were so or not, it is at least clear that the reiterated assurance of God to settle Israel by means of Joshua must have been a great source of strength to him.

The supreme inquiry for each of us, when summoned to a new work, is—not whether we possess sufficient strength or qualification for it, but—if we have been called to it by God; and when that is so there is no further cause for anxiety. If it is in his plan that we should march through a river, or attack a walled town, or turn to flight an army, we have simply to go forward. He will transform the mountains into a way. Rivers will dry up; walls will fall down; armies will be scattered as snow on Salmon (Ps. 68:14). There is no such thing as impossibility when God says, "Forward, soul: arise, go over this Jordan!"

3. THE SENSE OF THE PRESENCE OF GOD. "As I was with Moses, so I will be with thee. I will not fail thee, nor forsake thee." There was one particular in which Joshua would always come far behind his great predecessor. Both were in necessary and constant communication with God; but Joshua had to seek counsel through the high priest, whereas Moses had enjoyed direct intercourse with God, "speaking unto him face to face, as a man speaketh unto his friend" (Ex. 33:11). Still, Joshua the son of Nun was equally sure of the personal companionship of his great Ally, though he lacked the direct vision.

There have been generals whose presence on the field of battle has been the presage and guarantee of victory. Not only have they inspired the soldiers with a sense of confidence in their leadership, but they have encouraged them by their personal prowess and bravery. There is a marvelous sense of security and courage when a Christiana, a Mr. Fearing, or a Miss Much-afraid is assured of the presence of a Great-heart, who has never turned his back on a foe.* And a lonely, trembling soul dares to step bravely across the margin of life into the unknown beyond, to go down unabashed into the chill waters of death, because it can sing, "Thou art with me; thy rod and thy staff, they comfort me."

All through the arduous campaign that followed nothing

---

* In *Pilgrim's Progress, Part II.*

could daunt Joshua's courage while that assurance was ever ringing its silver tones in the belfry of his memory, "I will be with thee." Ah, it is well when we can so encourage ourselves in God! The fire is heated seven times; but he is with me, and no smell of fire shall pass upon my flesh. The river is deep; but he is with me, and its waters shall not sweep me off my feet. My enemies are many, and they hate me with cruel hatred; but he is with me, and no weapon that is formed against me shall prosper, and every tongue that shall rise in judgment against me he will condemn. Who can grow faint-hearted while he holds the right hand, saying, "Fear not, I am with thee!" The Lord Jesus ever lives to save unto the uttermost, and is with us all the days, even unto the end of the age.

4. THE INDWELLING OF THE WORD OF GOD. "This book of the law shall not depart out of thy mouth; but thou shalt meditate therein day and night." Words pass on to men the heroic thoughts which thrilled the souls of those who spoke them first. There are words, as there are strains of music, which cannot be uttered without nerving men to dare and do, to attempt and achieve. A woman will be strong to wait and suffer for long years on the strength of a sentence spoken by her lover as he parted from her. An army has before now forgotten sleepless nights and hungry marches in the stirring harangue of its general. Is not this what the prophet meant, when he said, "Thy words were found, and I did eat them; and thy word was unto me the joy and rejoicing of mine heart"? And is not this what Jesus meant when he said, "The words that I speak unto you, they are spirit, and they are life"?

We must meditate on the words of God, because it is through the Word of God that the Spirit of God comes in fullness to be the mighty occupant of our inner man. This, after all, is the secret of strength—to be possessed of the strong Son of God, strengthened by his indwelling might, and filled by his Spirit.

We can do all things when Christ is in us in unthwarted power. The only limit lies in our faith and capacity; or, in other words, in our absolute submission to his indwelling. Little children can overcome when there is within them One who is stronger than their foes. Weaklings may do exploits when the Mighty Conqueror who travels in the greatness of his strength makes them the vehicle of his progress. Nobodies, non-entities, broken reeds, bleached jawbones, quills plucked from wild fowl, and arrows that a babe could snap, accomplish marvels—because they are the channels through which the mysterious current of divine power from the Godhead flows forth to the world.

Our risen Lord is charged with power. It is stored in him for us as in a cistern. As the force of the brain is communicated to the members by the energy of the vital current flashing along the nerves, so does the power of Jesus come to us, his members, by the Holy Spirit. And if we would have that blessed Spirit we must seek him, not only in the fervid meeting or in the great convocation, but through the Word—wherein his force is stored.

Meditate on it day and night, till it yields to you strength and good courage, drawn from the nature of the glorified Redeemer. Your God has commanded your strength: claim it from Jesus through faith, by his Spirit, and in his Word.

Be strong in your weakness through the strengthening might of Christ. Take weakness, weariness, faint-heartedness, and difficulty into His presence; they will melt as hoarfrost in sunbeams. Give yourself wholly up to him, to do or die, as he shall choose. Then anoint your head, and wash your face. You shall have your inheritance in Timnath-heres (the portion of the sun). You shall make your way prosperous, and have good success. And you shall lead a nation to inherit the Land of Promise.

3

A THREE-DAY PAUSE

(JOSHUA 1:11–2:24)

"God's fashion is another: day by day,
And year by year, he tarrieth; little need
The Lord should hasten."
MYERS

THE whole land of Canaan was Israel's by deed of
gift. As soon as Lot had separated from Abraham,
choosing all the plain of Jordan, and pitching his tent
toward Sodom, the Lord drew near his faithful servant,
assuring him that he would not allow him to lose by his
magnanimity. "Arise," said the divine voice. "Walk
through the land in the length of it, and in the breadth
of it; for *I will give it unto thee*." But, after that, when
Melchizedek had blessed him and he had watched
through the long hours with God, beneath the horror of
the great darkness, "The Lord made a covenant with
him, saying, Unto thy seed *have I given this land*, from
the river of Egypt unto the great river, the river
Euphrates."

But though this was so, each square mile of it had to
be claimed from the hand of the peoples that possessed
it. "The sole of the foot" had to be put down to claim and
take. The cities were theirs, but they must enter them;

the houses which they had not built were theirs, but they must inhabit them; the wheatfields in the rich valleys and the vineyards on the terraced slopes were theirs, but they must possess them. It is not difficult for us to realize these things, for spiritually we occupy precisely a similar position. God our Father has blessed us with all spiritual blessings in Christ Jesus; but they are not ours to enjoy until we have claimed and appropriated them by a living faith. They are only ours as we avail ourselves of them. Hence the need to "be strong and very courageous."

But now a new and unexpected delay took place. A three-day pause was called for. The officers informed the people that three days must pass before they could go in to possess the land which the Lord their God was giving them to possess.

1. WHAT THIS PAUSE MEANT. "Three days" is a recognized period in Scripture for death and resurrection. "As Jonah was three days and three nights in the belly of the sea-monster (R.V. margin), so shall the Son of Man be three days and three nights in the heart of the earth." "On the third day he will raise us up, and we shall live before him." It was, therefore, appropriate that this period should elapse before the people could pass through symbolic death over to resurrection ground.

But there was another and deeper reason for the delay, which closely touches one of the greatest principles of the inner life. When Israel reached its banks, the Jordan was in flood, and overflowing the low-lying lands on either side of its bed. It was the time of "the swellings of Jordan," which in after-days was employed as an expression for overwhelming trouble. Before the gaze of the assembled hosts the turbid floods rushed on, swollen by melting snows far away on Hermon, and carrying trunks of trees and other debris torn from the banks in their impetuous descent. Its force and velocity, as it poured down from its upper basins to the immense depression of the Dead Sea, had gained for it the name of "Descender"; and this title was especially appropriate at such seasons as that at which Israel first beheld it.

Across the river stood Jericho, embosomed in palms and tamarisks, in a very paradise of exquisite vegetation, its aromatic shrubs and gardens scenting the air. But as the people beheld it, all their cherished hopes of taking it by their own energy or courage must have been utterly dissipated. What could they do in face of that broad expanse of rushing, foaming, turbulent waters? The Jordan, on the page of Scripture, is constantly associated with death. This indeed is its common characteristic. Not the death of the body; but that baptism into death which signifies a pause in the energies of nature, and an entrance through faith on a higher and nobler level. So John baptized there; and there the Lord entered into his first identification with sins not his own. But never in all its history did the Jordan more effectually pronounce the sentence of death than on that day when it taught the people that by no strength or energy of their own could they prevail.

Multitudes have come to the brink of that river, and have been left there, waiting on its banks, that they might consider the meaning of those impassable waters, and carry away the sentence of death in themselves. Abraham waited there for more than twenty years, face to face with the apparent impossibility of ever having a son. David waited there for almost as long; and it must have seemed that the kingdom foretold to him as a youth lay on the other side of insurmountable difficulties. The sisters of Bethany waited there; and the stone, rolled heavily to the door of the tomb where Lazarus lay, must have been to them all that the Jordan was to Israel—the knell of hope.

Many a saint since then has been brought down to these same banks, and has stood to witness this flowing stream. Even though the promise of God has offered all manner of blessedness and delight, there is that river—always that river! That flooded, fordless, bridgeless, boatless river! Are you there now, my reader? Do not hasten from it. Stand still and consider, until the energy and impetuosity of your self-life dies down. You can never reach the Blessed Life by resolutions, or pledges, or forms of covenant; your good self is as powerless now as your bad self was formerly. You must learn that your strength is to sit still, and that the rich blessings of God stored in Christ for you are an absolute gift to be received by the outstretched hand of faith.

What a marvelous expression that is concerning the faith of Abraham! "Without being weakened in faith, he considered his own body as good as dead, and the deadness of Sarah's womb" (Rom. 4:19, R.V.). Not many could have long stood such considerations without losing all the faith they ever possessed. There was one secret, however, that sustained him. "He looked unto the promise of God." Turning from the one to the other, he wavered not. These are the only conditions on which the vision of the river will not hurt us; if only we turn from it to the presence of the Captain of the Lord's host, and to the covenant which is ordered in all things and sure. Then we shall grow strong through faith, and be fully assured that what God has promised he is able also to perform.

2. HOW THIS PAUSE WAS SPENT. During this space of three days events transpired which are both interesting and typical. Among other things, Jericho was entered by the two spies.

(a) Jericho may aptly stand for the world of men over which judgment is impending, but which goes on its way unheeding. The blue sky spread its canopy overhead; the sun rose and set; the fields were ripened for harvest; the vintage was preparing; youth and beauty with linked hands pursued a flower-strewn path. But within a fortnight a blow was to fall from which the city would not rally for centuries.

The great majority of the people were either bent on stubborn resistance or boasted themselves on their river and their walls. Their iniquity was full. And no proclamation was made to them, no terms proposed, no embassy sent. But there was one soul in their midst who was capable of faith, and was already exercising it. And he who had nurtured Rahab and led her to the point which she had reached was bent on perfecting what he had commenced, and on leading her into the fullest light which that age possessed. This is ever God's way. If there is but one righteous person in Sodom, he cannot destroy the city till his angels have brought him forth. If there is but one doubter among the apostles, he will not leave him comfortless, but will come to him with unmistakable tokens. Wherever there is a Rahab who, amid much sin and ignorance, is living up to the truth she has, and longs for more, God will take her hand and lead her to himself. He discerns a touch on his robe, and stays his footsteps till he has fully healed. A Nathanael beneath the fig tree, a eunuch in his chariot, a Cornelius praying beside the sea, are not overlooked amid the crowds of careless souls around. They are as jewels on a heap of cinders, which are eagerly espied and taken up, polished, and placed amid the divine regalia.

Two references are made in the New Testament to Rahab's faith (Heb. 11:31; James 2:25). It was true faith, though exercised only toward a fragment of the truth. It is not the amount of truth that a man holds which saves him but the grasp with which he holds it. All that Rahab knew was that God had delivered his people from Pharaoh, and had promised to give them that land; and she believed it: and it was accounted to her for righteousness. And the evidences of her faith were quick to follow. She came into antagonism with the world-spirit as represented in the king of Jericho; she sent the spies out by another way. She identified herself with Israel by the scarlet thread; she gathered her kinsfolk under her roof; her window looked toward Israel, while her door stood open to shelter many a fugitive. And though her faith was not as yet sufficiently strong to deliver her entirely from the fear of man which brought the snare of lying, yet she was commended to the care of Israel, and became a link in the ancestry of the Son of Man.

Rahab, the poor outcast of Jericho, who had this strange faith in God, entered in with the people to possess the land that flowed with milk and honey. She is thus the type of Gentile sinners who are permitted to share in the unsearchable riches of Christ; to sit with him in the heavenlies; to form part of that new race which is gathering around the true Joshua, the Lord from heaven. We were not a people; but we are now the people of God. We had not obtained mercy; but we have now obtained it. We were far off; but we are now made nigh by the blood of Christ. So then we are no more strangers or sojourners; but we are fellow citizens with the saints, and of the household of God. Only let us avail ourselves of our heritage!

(b) During this brief pause Joshua also had an opportunity of ascertaining the feelings of the two and a half tribes. He discovered that they were fully prepared to discharge the obligation into which they had entered with Moses, and to march with the other tribes to the conquest of Canaan. But they were equally set on returning to the rich pasture lands of Gilead and Bashan, which Moses had given them beyond Jordan, toward the sunrising. They had "much cattle" (Num. 32:2, 4, 19, 33).

Are not these the type of Christians to whom the Land of Promise is as freely open as to others, and who make an incursion into it with no thought of remaining? They are willing to pit their strength against the seven nations of Canaan, but they are not prepared to abandon the strong fascinations of the world, and to settle down to a life hidden with Christ in God. Are there not among us those who have spent seven years in the Land of Promise and have had hallowed experiences of blessedness, rest, and power, but who have been swept off their feet and back by the advancing tide of worldliness?

The end of such is but too clearly suggested by the fate of those Eastern tribes. They had their much grass; but they became gradually cut off from the corporate life of Israel. They gave few great names to the roll of saints and heroes emblazoned on Israel's story. They were the first to fall beneath the heel of Assyria, and were swept into captivity, from which they never returned.

From such a lot may we all be saved! Rather be it our happy portion to be employed as the Lord's ambassadors in seeking souls; shown where to find them; taught how to deal with them; and enabled to lead them out into complete identification with the people of God.

3. HOW THE PAUSE ENDED. On the third day the hosts seem to have come nearer the river's brink, and their tents were pitched for the night within close proximity to the hurrying waters. It was then that Joshua said unto the people, "Sanctify yourselves; for tomorrow the Lord will do wonders among you." From which it would seem that the wonder-working power of God is dependent upon the sanctification of his people. When we ask the ancient question, "Why art thou as a mighty man that cannot save?" (Jer. 14:9), we get the answer— which shows that *we* are to blame for the divine impotence— "He could do no mighty works there, *because of their unbelief.*"

We all want to see wonders wrought by God—in our own characters, that the fir tree may replace the thorn, and the myrtle the brier; in our homes, that the desert places may blossom with roses; in our churches, that they may arise and put on their beautiful garments. Oh for another Pentecost! Oh for a widespread revival of true godliness! Oh for the making bare of the right hand of the Most High! Oh to see converts fly as doves to their windows! And why is it that we strain our eyes for them in vain? Is it not because we have not sanctified ourselves? Sanctification means the cleansing of the soul, and the putting on of the white robes of purity and humility. We are not clean enough for God to use us. We are not humble enough to bear a great success. It is perfectly true that we can only be wholly sanctified by the God of Peace. Holiness on its positive side is his indwelling and filling; but on its negative side it involves the putting away of known sin, or our willing that he should cleanse it away from us by blood, or water, or fire.

Is this our condition? Have we laid aside our weights as well as our sins? Are we cleansed from all filthiness of the flesh and spirit? Are we able to say with the apostle that we do not condemn ourselves in anything that we allow? If not, let us no longer complain that the days of wonders are over. We are ourselves accountable for their having vanished, like peace from the criminal, and purity from the fallen. No wonder we are always dreading tomorrow. Tomorrow with God, and without the wonders of his mighty arm, is indeed a dismal outlook.

But if only each one of us were to sanctify himself— putting off the old man with his deeds and putting on the new man, renewed daily in the image of Christ; forsaking every form of evil, and hating even the garment spotted by the flesh; yielding himself to the two-edged sword of the great High Priest—we should find that wonders would begin and never cease; that the tomorrows would only unfold greater and better things than ever before; that Jordans would cleave and Jerichos would fall. Then the Land of Promise would lie open with its immeasurable plenty, its oil and wine, its corn and honey—its precious, priceless stores.

4

CROSSING THE JORDAN

(JOSHUA 3:10)

"Omnipotence is on your side,
    And Wisdom watches o'er your heads,
And God himself will be your Guide,
    So ye but follow where he leads:
How many, guided by his hand,
Have reached ere now their fatherland!
    Press on! press on!"

LEHR

THE words "I will drive out" are familiar ones in the Mosaic record of the Exodus. A dozen times at least God promised, through his servant, to drive out the nations of Canaan before his people. Sometimes it was to be wrought by sending an angel, and sometimes a hornet; for though God's righteous acts are fair and lovely to his children, they are terrible to his adversaries. All that Israel had to do was to march straight before them into the Land of Promise, and they would find that kings would quickly flee, and the mightiest armies would retreat in panic.

There were several reasons why it was needful for God to drive out the seven nations which dwelt in Canaan. But chief among them stands that suggested by the memorable interview held between Jehovah and

Abraham, the ancestor of the chosen race, four centuries before—the iniquity of the Amorites was now full (Gen. 15:16).

In the first place, the nations of Canaan had abandoned themselves to *the most abominable immorality.* After enumerating several impure actions, which were not to be so much as named among the chosen people, Moses, speaking as the mouthpiece of Jehovah, said, "Defile not ye yourselves in any of these things; for in all these the nations are defiled which I cast out before you, and the land is defiled: therefore do I visit the iniquity thereof upon it, and the land itself vomiteth out her inhabitants" (Lev. 19:24–25). The destruction of the people by the sword of Israel was only the hastening of the natural results of their shameful vice. The reasons which necessitated the Deluge of water necessitated this deluge of blood. Plague-spot as it was, Canaan would have infected the world had it not been passed through the fire.

In the second place, the Canaanites were *steeped in spiritualism,* and held close communication with the demons of the air, which has always been forbidden to men. On the eve of Israel's entrance into Canaan, Moses said, "There shall not be found with thee one that useth divination, one that practiceth augury, or an enchanter, or a sorcerer, or a charmer, or a consulter with a familiar spirit, or a wizard, or a necromancer. For whosoever doeth these things is an abomination unto the Lord; and because of these abominations the Lord thy God doth drive them out from before thee" (Deut. 18:10–12). These terms include mesmerism; the use of evil spirits to get aid and information; demoniacal possession of bodies of mediums; and the apparent summoning back of the departed. "All these things are a transgression of the limits of humanity as laid down by the Creator. And the unlawful confusion brings its own immediate punishment, in addition to the fearful judgment to come.

For our body appears to be intended to serve as a fortress; and is not improbably devised for the very purpose of sheltering us in some degree from the corrupting influence of demons" (Pember). When, therefore, man breaks through this strong fence, and opens a passage of communication with the fallen spirits around, he exposes himself to God's direst wrath; and for the sake of the race these black arts must be stayed.

And this last thought gives a new complexion to this conflict. In driving out and destroying these demoralized races, God was in effect waging war with the evil spirits, who from their seat in the heavenlies were ruling the darkness of that land. This conflict was not against flesh and blood, "but against the principalities, against the powers, against the spiritual hosts of wickedness in the heavenly places." The mighty armies marshaled against Israel were dissipated as chaff before the breeze of the summer evening because the demons whom they worshiped were being driven out before the Lord's host, the Captain of which appeared presently to Joshua. At this time, probably, to celestial watchers, Satan appeared to fall as lightning from heaven. And thus this old record is invested with a new interest. It is not simply the story of the conquest of Canaan; it is a fragment from the chronicles of heaven, giving an episode in the eternal conflict between light and darkness, between heaven and hell, between the Son of God and his great antagonist, the devil. What an interesting additional analogy is presented by this fact, linking the Book of Joshua and the Epistle to the Ephesians!

God graciously gave a sign regarding the ultimate issue of the war, so that through the seven years of coming conflict the people of Israel might be at rest as to the result. "Hereby ye shall know that the living God is among you, and that he will without fail drive out from before you the Canaanites, and the Hittites, and the Hivites, and the Perizzites, and the Girgashites, and the

Amorites, and the Jebusites. Behold, the ark of the covenant of the Lord of all the earth passeth over before you into Jordan." The passage through the turbulent waters of the Jordan was to be the Heaven-appointed sign: just as the passage of our Lord through death, his resurrection, and his ascension, are the Heaven-appointed signs that he shall at last put down all rule, and authority, and power, destroy the works of the devil, and give up the kingdom to God, even the Father.

1. THE CROSSING OF THE JORDAN. At the close of the three days of preparation there seems to have been a movement of the camp from Shittim, with its acacia groves, to a spot within a mile of the boisterous rush of the swollen river. There Israel spent the last memorable night of pilgrimage and wandering. As the dawn broke, the officers again passed through the host, and bade the people watch and follow the movements of the ark. A short interval only would elapse before the congregation had struck their slight, black tents, packed up their household goods, adjusted their burdens, and stood in one great host, two and a half million strong, prepared to tread the untried path—the way that they had not passed heretofore—though it led into the valley of death. The sun was rising behind them, its beams flashing on the Jordan, a mile of water broad, and setting in bold relief the white walls of the houses of Jericho; while all the adjacent hills of Canaan stood around veiled in morning mist, or robed in the exquisite garments of light.

At last a little group emerged from those densely crowded hosts. It was the chosen band of priests, white-robed, barefooted, who slowly descended the terraced bank of the river, bearing on their shoulders the sacred ark, its golden lid and bending cherubim hidden beneath their covering of blue. How awful the silence! How fixed the gaze that followed them every step! How hushed the voices of wiseacres and gainsayers who had been loud all the previous days in protesting that the passage was impossible, and that it would be wiser to wait until the mile of water had dwindled to the normal width of thirty yards when the stream was four or six feet deep, and easily fordable!

Nearer the little procession went; but even when it was within a yard of the river brink, its approach effected nothing. The waters showed no disposition to flee or fail. But when the feet of the priests were dipped into the tiny wavelets, brown with mud, yeasty with the foam of their hurried rush, a marvelous change took place. They began to divide and shrink away. And as the priests pursued them, descending ever farther toward the midst of Jordan, they fled before them as if panic-stricken. "What ailed thee, thou Jordan, that thou turnedst back?" Nothing could account for so great a wonder, save the presence of the God of Jacob, and that the ark of the covenant of the Lord of all the earth was passing through those depths.

Far up the river, at a distance of some thirty miles, at Adam, the city that is beside Zaretan, the flow of the river had suddenly been stopped, and the waters, unable to hurry forward, gathered into a heap, and probably formed a vast lake that spread itself for miles. From that point and downward, the waters, no longer supplied from above, began to fail; they hurried toward the Sea of Death, and were swallowed up in its dark, unwholesome depths. "They were wholly cut off." And as there were none to follow, the riverbed for miles was dry; and the people, hurrying down the bank, "hastened and passed over."

Mark the all-inclusiveness of the miracle. It did not concern the strong only, but also the weak; not men only, but women and children; not the loyal and true only, but the querulous, the murmurers, the doubters, the fearless and unbelieving. Achan, whose heart was preparing for his deed of sin; and Caleb, the hale warrior, who wholly followed the Lord. Not one was missing. The feet of the priests stood firm till every individual of the redeemed race had crossed the river. It is a blessed anticipation of the keeping back of a more awful flood until without one exception the entire host of the Church has entered that city whose walls are Salvation, and its gates Praise.

And this was the promised sign. For he who could drive out the waters would drive out their foes. Having done so much, he would complete that which he had begun. No child of the kingdom may put his hand to the plow and then look back; how much less the King himself.

2. THE TYPICAL SIGNIFICANCE OF THIS CROSSING. The Son of God was manifested that he might destroy the works of the devil. The dispossession of the devil from the position which he has usurped is as certain as that of the Canaanites from the Land of Promise. His doom is sure. He must be cast out. Our Emmanuel will not fail nor be discouraged until our great enemy and all his armies have been cast out of the heavenlies into the earth, and out of the earth into the abyss, and thence into the lake of fire. And this is the sign of it, that he dipped his feet in death: and, dying, abolished death. It fled before him, as Jordan before the priests; and for those who live and believe in him, though the semblance of dying remains, it is as a riverbed from which the water has shrunk away, and the blood-bought go over dry shod.

Christian people do not seem to understand this glorious fact. They think that death to them will be much as it has been and is to the myriads who die out of Christ. But surely this is a profound mistake. When Jesus died, he entirely altered the article of death for all who believe. "Through death he brought to naught him that had the power of death, that is the devil; and delivered them who through fear of death were all their lifetime subject to bondage" (Heb. 2:14–15, R.V.).

In view of these considerations what a ray of light flashes on several of these sentences!

"*There shall be a space between you and the ark.*" Yes, the Lord Jesus preceded his Church. He first passed through the grave in resurrection power. "Every man in his own order: Christ the firstfruits, afterward they that are Christ's." In all things, and therefore in this also, he must have the preeminence. When he putteth forth his own sheep, he goeth before them; and his sheep follow him. "The breaker is gone up before them: they have broken forth and passed on to the gate, and are gone out thereat, and their king is passed on before them, and the Lord at the head of them" (Micah 2:13, R.V.).

"*And the Lord said unto Joshua, This day will I begin to magnify thee.*" And surely the exaltation of Christ as the God-man dates from the moment that he stepped into the hurrying waters of death and dried them up. "The God of Peace brought again from the dead our Lord Jesus, that great Shepherd of the Sheep, through the blood of the everlasting covenant."

"*The priests that bare the ark of the covenant of the Lord stood firm until all the nation were passed clean over Jordan.*" Thus does the merit of Jesus avail

"Till all the ransomed Church of God
Be saved to sin no more."

The waters of judgment may be accumulating for all who cling to the old Adam-stock; but they can never slip from their leash until every trembling, laggard soul that will has passed into blessed rest. You may be young, or crippled, or ready to give up, or much afraid; but if you will but cast in your lot with the host of the ransomed, the Priest will lengthen out the dispensation, and hold the waters back for you.

"*The people hasted and passed over.*" Not that they were afraid of being caught in the rush of water; but that they might not overtire the waiting priests, patiently standing, the precious burden on their shoulders. Has not the patience of Jesus been greatly exercised during these long centuries? He longs to take his bride to himself, to reap the harvest of his tears, and see the fruit of the travail of his soul. Let us hasten the coming of the day of God, by learning all his holy lessons, doing his blessed will, and hastening the Lots that linger at the gates of Sodom.

Here, then, is the blessed sign of the final victory of the Son of God; and every Christian who passes into the Land of Promise, Rest, and Victory, who begins to live the resurrection life, who knows what it is to stand in conscious rapture of power, is another pledge that before long the song shall be heard ringing through all the spheres: "Hallelujah! the kingdoms of this world have become the kingdoms of our God and of his Christ, and he shall reign forever."

3. THE BEARING OF THIS CROSSING ON CHRISTIAN EXPERIENCE.

(*a*) We have already seen the effect produced by the death of the Lord Jesus on death. It is appointed unto man once to die. And since we have died in him, we shall find death robbed of its terrors. The darkness of the valley is only that of a shadow. But this is not all. By virtue of our union with him, we have passed through death on to resurrection ground, and have become "the children of the resurrection." It is on this fact in our spiritual history that the apostles base many of their most powerful arguments and appeals. "We who died to sin, how shall we any longer live therein?" "Ye were made dead to the law, through the body of Christ, that ye should be joined to another, even to him who was raised from the dead." "Forasmuch then as Christ suffered in the flesh, arm ye yourselves also with the same mind; for he that hath suffered in the flesh hath ceased from sin; that ye no longer should live the rest of your time to the lusts of men, but to the will of God" (1 Pet. 4:1–2, R.V.).

(*b*) With this truth we can foil the most bewitching

fascinations of the world. We have passed out of it with our dear Lord. We have left it behind us on the other side of his grave. We cannot love that which crucified him, and us in him. We have died, and our life is hid with Christ in God. We have risen, and seek those things which are above, where Christ is seated at the right hand of God. We have become citizens of the new Jerusalem; and if we still move amid the world's attractions, it is in the garb of strangers and foreigners—men from the other side of the river, who speak the language and wear the attire of the heavenly Canaan—the language, *love;* the attire, *the white raiment,* pure and clean, washed in the Blood of the Lamb.

It is true that Jordans always roll between us and our Canaans. We are permitted to catch glimpses of spiritual experience which is not only within our reach but evidently intended for us. A face lighted up with an unearthly glow; a recital of an experience; a passage in a book; a text; a sermon—these have revealed something as radiant to our gaze as Jericho must have seemed to those weary travelers. But there is a Jordan between us and it. And the turbulent waters seem an impassible barrier.

There is no hope that we shall be able to cope with these things by any might or wisdom of our own. As well might we seek to arrest a river in its flood, or curb the ocean in storm. The opposition of that relative; the hatred of that persecutor; the strength of that passion; the tyranny of that habit; the untowardness of our circumstances—these are our Jordan. How easy life would be if only these were other than they are! Give me Canaan without its Jordan! But God permits the Jordans that he may educate our faith. Do not look at the troubled waters rushing past; look at the Priest, who is also the Ark of the Covenant. He will never send us by a way that he is not willing to tread before us. "Behold, the ark of the covenant of the Lord of all the earth passeth over before you into Jordan."

Keep in living fellowship with the Apostle and High Priest of your profession. Consider him. Look away from all else to him. Follow him. It may seem as if he is leading you into certain destruction; but it shall not be so. When you come to the dreaded difficulty, be it what it may, you will find that because his feet have been dipped in its brink, it has dwindled in its flow. Its roar is hushed; its waters are shrunken; its violence is gone. The iron gate stands open. The stone is rolled from the sepulcher. The riverbed is dry. Jericho is within reach. "They passed over right against Jericho."

5

THE STONES OF GILGAL

(JOSHUA 4 AND 5)

"Less, less of self each day,
    And more, my God, of thee!
Oh, keep me in the way,
    However rough it be!
Leave naught that is unmeet;
    Of all that is mine own
Strip me; and so complete
    My training for the throne."

                              H. BONAR

ON the western side of Jordan, to which the host of Israel had now come, five miles from the river brink, the terraced banks reached their highest point. That was Gilgal. There the first camp was pitched, on the edge of a vast grove of majestic palms, nearly three miles broad and eight miles long, that stretched away to Jericho. Dean Stanley suggests that, as Joshua witnessed it, it must have recalled to him the magnificent palm-groves of Egypt, such as stretch at the present day along the shores of the Nile at Memphis. Amidst this forest could have been seen, reaching through its open spaces, fields of ripe grain, "for it was the time of the barley harvest"; and above the topmost trees the high walls and towers of the city on the farther side, which from that grove derived its proud name, "Jericho, the City of Palms."

Gilgal was the base of operations in the war against the people of Canaan. There the camp remained, and the women and children (9:6; 10:6). It ranked with Mizpeh and Bethel among the holy places, where Samuel exercised his sacred office (1 Sam. 7:16). It was the rallying point to which the people gathered at solemn times of national crisis (11:4). Saul had reason to remember it; and there Agag was hewed in pieces "before the Lord."

Probably to the last of the events, and beyond, the twelve stones were visible which had been pitched by Joshua as the lasting memorial of the passage of the river. Children were brought thither by their parents to see them, and to hear the wondrous story of the passage, recited on the spot in words which Joshua had suggested long before.

At the time when the book was written, the other heap of stones, laid in the riverbed, must have been clearly discernible whenever the stream, after being swollen by the spring floods, had retreated to its normal width (4:9); and there could have been no difficulty in fixing the hill of circumcision, where, at the command of God, they had rolled away the reproach of Egypt, and from which the name Gilgal, or Rolling, was derived (5:9).

Gilgal was from the first "holy ground" (5:15); and as we traverse it again in devout thought, it will give us also themes for deep and holy meditation.

1. THE STONES ON THE BANK. At the divine bidding, twelve men, one out of each tribe, went down into the river's bed on a special errand. From the place where the priests' feet stood firm in Jordan they took each man a stone. It may be that the priests had selected those stones as providing a safe and secure footing; or perhaps they lay within some short distance of the spot where they had stood upbearing the sacred symbol of the presence of God. For centuries these stones had lain

there undisturbed; but now, piled together in a heap before the eyes of all men, they were to be a memorial of the passage of Jordan, as the song of Moses was of the passage through the Red Sea.

It is well that forgetful hearts like ours should be stirred up by way of remembrance. We are so apt to grow unmindful of the Rock that begat us, and to forget the God that gave us birth. Even the Lord, whose love effected a redemption which runs parallel with our lives, as a river beside a carriage road, needed to set up a memorial of his most precious death on our behalf. There is, therefore, a need for these memorial stones to be erected beside our Jordans, with their inscription, "Wherefore remember."

The special circumstance which these stones commemorated was that they had come, a united people, through the Jordan; and that as a nation they had been brought into the land promised to their fathers. What though two and a half tribes had elected to stay with their cattle in the rich pastures of Gilead and Bashan? They were still an integral part of the people. There were *twelve* stones. And in later centuries, if the heap remained intact, even after the northern tribes had been carried into captivity, any who came thither would be compelled to admit that there had been a time when the twelve tribes of Israel had stood together, on that spot, a united and mighty nation.

And what is the typical and spiritual significance of this? Why this reverent care to pitch these boulder stones, and to record with such minute detail the fact? What mean these stones? Those who have followed carefully the teaching of the preceding chapters cannot hesitate as to the reply. As in the passage of the Jordan all Israel came up onto the river's bank, so in the resurrection and ascension of the Lord Jesus the whole Church of his redeemed passed over to resurrection ground, and are, in the purpose and thought of God, already seated in the heavenlies.

There can be no doubt that this is the teaching of the Holy Spirit through the apostles. It comes out unmistakably in the writings of Peter as well as of Paul. No fact is better attested or more eagerly emphasized. To ignore it is to miss the foundation on which the structure of a full and present salvation is based. We must go back to the cross for the Atonement; but we must also go back to it for our passage in him to the resurrection side of death:

> "In him we died, in him we rose,
> In him we triumphed o'er our foes;
> In him in heaven we took our seat,
> And heaven rejoiced o'er earth's defeat."

It is in the Revised Version, with its more accurate rendering of the tenses of the original Greek, that this mighty fact stands out with most distinctness. Addressing those who at the time when the Lord Jesus was dying on the cross were probably living in the lusts of their flesh, doing the desires of the flesh and of the mind, the apostle says: "Even when we were dead through our trespasses, God quickened us together with Christ, and raised us up with him, and made us to sit with him in the heavenlies" (Eph. 2:5–6). And in each case the use of the aorist tense points to a definite past act by which their position, and that of the whole Church, was settled, once and for all, so far, at least, as the purpose and thought of God are concerned.

It cannot be too often or too clearly emphasized that the basic thought in the New Testament philosophy of deliverance from the power of sin consists in the intelligent apprehension of this divine fact—that the whole Church was identified with Jesus in his death, and resurrection, and ascension; that all died with him; all lay in his grave; all rose with him on the Easter morning; all passed with him, in the divine intention, to the throne. It was no lonely figure that, as the light of morning broke on the Temple dome, climbed the steeps of the sky, drawn by an invisible attraction; he was accompanied by a multitude which no man could have numbered. In him you and I and all believers trod down the principalities and powers of darkness, and took our place above them all. What though as yet for many of us this seems a dream? Yet let us never rest till the Spirit of God has made it a living fact. And let it be the one aim of our life by faith to make that true in daily life and experience which is true in the thought and purpose of our God.

Consider those twelve stones on the farther side of Jordan; and be sure that as they represented the entire people, and commemorated their marvelous transportation from the one side of Jordan to the other, so, in the New Jerusalem, the twelve foundation stones bearing the names of the apostles, and the twelve gates inscribed with the names of the twelve tribes of Israel, are a standing memorial that the Church as a whole is on resurrection ground; but her shame and sorrow are that she has not availed herself of her lofty privileges, or descended to earth as girded with the power of the risen, living Jesus.

We have crossed the River. Our eternity is begun. Part possession of our heritage has already been bestowed. In Jesus we are loved and accepted; we are more than conquerors; we occupy a position which, if only we keep it, is unassailable by our foes; they can only prevail against us when they succeed in tempting us to abandon it. All things are ours in union with our raised and reigning Lord; whether the world, or life, or death, or things present or things to come—all are ours, and we are Christ's, and Christ is God's.

2. THE STONES IN THE BED OF THE STREAM. Not content with pitching a cairn of stones on the river's bank, Joshua, at God's command, set up twelve stones in the midst of Jordan, in the place where the feet of the

priests that bore the ark of the covenant stood. And often, as he came back and again to Gilgal, he must have gone out by himself to walk and muse beside the river, turning the outward and the inner gaze to the spot where beneath the flow of the current those stones lay hidden. They were the lasting memorial of the miracle which otherwise might have faded from memory, or seemed incredible. They were aids to faith. Where they lay, the people had been, and the feet of the priests had been planted dry. And surely the power that had arrested the Jordan, and brought the people up from its bed, would not fail until it had wrought out the whole purpose of God.

We too may often walk along that river, and gaze into those depths. There Jesus lay in death for us, and there we lay in him; and not we only, but all his Church. "For if one died for all, then all died." Each time we partake of the Lord's Supper, or behold the rite of baptism administered in the form of immersion, or fall into the ground to die in acts of self-sacrifice and self-dying, we stand with Joshua beside the Jordan, covering the twelve memorial stones; and there float through our thought, like a strain of thrilling music, the words, "Now that he ascended, what is it but that he also descended first into the lower parts of the earth, . . . that he might fill all things."

Nothing breaks the power of sin like this. When we apprehend the love of Christ and the meaning of his death, we are constrained to live no longer to ourselves, but to him. By his cross we too have been crucified to the world, and the world to us. Other men may be fascinated by the lust of the flesh, the lust of the eyes, and the pride of life; but these things have lost their charm for us. How can we love them when we remember what they did unto our Lord—our life, our love, the bridegroom and husband of our souls? What true woman can dally with the murderer of her spouse?

Go, O Christian soul, and meditate long and prayerfully on this great spiritual fact. Realize that you have passed into another sphere. You have been released by the death of your first husband, the Law; and you are married to another, even to him who was raised from the dead. You share his life, his home, his protection. That principle of sin that held you fast in the lower sphere may not follow you here. Death bars its way. Reckon, then, yourself to be dead indeed to sin, but alive to God in Christ Jesus; and answer every solicitation of the world, the flesh, the devil, by affirming that you are none of theirs.

Let us also remember that the very same power, "the working of the strength of his might," which availed to raise Christ, our representative and head, from the grave, and to set him far above all orders of spiritual beings at the Father's right hand, is available for each of us who believe. Electricity lay hidden around men in those long ages in which they were oblivious to its presence and unable to apply it to their needs; and God's mighty resurrection energy lies all around us, waiting for us to avail ourselves of it. Let us claim and appropriate and use it, yielding ourselves to its impulses, and learning that there is nothing in the purpose of God which he is not prepared to make true in the happy experience of those who believe.

3. THE RITE OF CIRCUMCISION. Israel looked for nothing less than to be led from the river brink to the conquest and partition of the land. They suddenly discovered, however, that this was not quite the divine program for them. Rather, they were required to submit to a painful rite, the seal of the covenant which was made originally to Abraham, and by virtue of which the land had been given to him and to his seed (Gen. 17:8–10).

During the wanderings of the desert—which were due to their unbelief, and practically disinherited them—the observance of this rite had been in abeyance, because

SUSPENSION

the operation of the covenant was, for the time, in suspense. But now that the new young nation was learning to exercise its faith, the covenant and its seal came again into operation. "Their children, whom he raised up in their stead, them did Joshua circumcise."

Even those comparatively unenlightened people must have realized that there was deep spiritual significance in the administration of that rite at that juncture. On more than one occasion they had heard Moses speak of circumcising the heart; and they must have felt that God meant to teach them the vanity of trusting to their numbers, or prowess, or martial array. Their strength was nothing to him. The land was not to be won by their might, but to be taken from his hand as a gift. Self and the energy of the flesh must be set aside, that the glory of coming victory might be of God, and not of man.

We, too, must have our Gilgal. It is not enough to acknowledge as a general principle that we are dead and risen with Christ; we must apply it to our inner and outer life. If we died with Christ, we must mortify our members, which are upon the earth. If we put away the old man with his doings, in our profession, we must also put away anger, wrath, malice, railing, and shameful speaking. If we were raised together with Christ, we must seek those things which are above, where Christ is seated on the right hand of God. The first effect of our appreciation of the meaning of Christ's death will be our application of that death to our members which are upon the earth. We have no warrant to say that sin is dead, or that the principle of sin is eradicated; but that we are dead to it in our standing, and are dead to it also in the reckoning of faith.

But for this we need the gift of the Blessed Spirit, in his Pentecostal fullness. It was by the Eternal Spirit that our Lord offered himself in death upon the cross; and it is by him alone that we can mortify the deeds of the body. For, first, the spirit of self is so subtle. It is like a taint in the blood, which, stayed in one place, breaks out in another. Protean in its shapes and ubiquitous in its hiding places, it requires omniscience to discover and omnipresence to expel. And, secondly, only the Spirit of God has cords strong enough to bind us to the altar of death; to remind us in the hour of temptation; to enable us to look to Jesus for his grace; to inspire us with the passion of self-immolation; to keep us true and steady to the resolves of our holiest moments; to apply the withering fire of the cross of Jesus to the growth of our self-conceit and self-energy—for all these the grace of the Spirit is indispensable. He is the Spirit of life in Christ Jesus, therefore he must be the Spirit of death to all that pertains to the old Adam.

There is a sense in which all believers have been circumcised in Christ; but there is another sense in which it is needful for them to pass one after another through the circumcision of Christ which is not made with hands, and which consists in the putting off of the body of the flesh. To that all who would lead a life of victory and inherit the Land of Promise must submit. The process may be sharp, for the knife does not spare pain. But it is in the hands of Jesus, the Lover of souls. Oh, shrink not from it! Let him do all that he deems needful, though it takes many days till the wound is healed.

At first it might appear strange that the past experience of resurrection life should lead to death. But on further reflection it is not hard to see that all which is of the flesh must be condemned and executed even as he was, who came in the likeness of sinful flesh, that the ordinance of the law might be fulfilled in us who walked not after the flesh but after the Spirit. And though it might appear that the circumcised life will ever be a maimed life, it is not really so; the contrary is the universal testimony of this book. When the hand is cut off, we go maimed *into life*. When we mortify the deeds of the body, we begin to live. When the Lord our God has circumcised our hearts, then we love him with all our heart and with all our soul—and we live.

You can never take Jericho, Christian worker, till you have been circumcised, till God has taken away your self-reliance, and has brought you down into the dust of death; then, when the sentence of death is in yourself, you will begin to experience the energy of the divine life, the glory of the divine victory.

6

THREE SUCCESSIVE DAYS

(JOSHUA 5:10–12)

> "To feed on Christ is to get his strength into us to be our
> strength. You feed on the cornfield, and the strength of the
> cornfield comes into you, and is your strength. You feed on
> Christ, and then go and live your life; and it is Christ in you
> that lives your life, that helps the poor, that tells the truth,
> that fights the battle, and that wins the crown."
>
> PHILLIPS BROOKS

IN one of his sonnets, Matthew Arnold tells of an
interview he had on a day of fierce August sunshine,
in Bethnal Green, with a preacher whom he knew, and
who looked ill and overworked. In answer to the inquiry
as to how he fared:

"Bravely!" said he; "for I of late have been much
cheered with thoughts of Christ, the *Living Bread*." He is
not the only human soul who, above the ebb and flow of
London storm and tumult, has set up a mark of everlasting light to cheer and to right his course through the
night. For holy souls have ever loved to meditate upon
that wonderful power which they possess, of absorbing
into themselves the very nature of him who, though he
was the Everlasting Son of the Father, became man,
that the forces of deity might through him pass out to

those who love him.

There is a great difference between the strength which may be supplied from without and that which is assimilated within. To illustrate the first: we tread the cathedral close and examine the mighty buttresses that steady the ancient walls. Even though the high, embowed roof presses on them with all its weight to make them bulge, they cannot stir an inch from the perpendicular so long as those masses of stone, built up without, forbid. To illustrate the second: we must visit the forest glade, where giant oaks withstand the blasts of centuries because they have incorporated into their hearts the properties of earth and air, becoming robust and sturdy and storm-defying.

There are many ways in which the holy soul derives strength from without. It is buttressed by remonstrances and appeals; by providences and promises; by the fear of causing grief; and by the incitement of passionate devotion. But if these were all, they would be insufficient. We need to have within ourselves the strong Son of God; to know that the Mightiest is within us, working through us, so that we, even as he, can do all things.

In this old record we may discover without effort the Living Bread under three aspects: the Passover, the produce of the land, and the manna. Each of these was associated with one of three successive days.

1. THE PASSOVER. The Passover itself could never be repeated: once for all it lay back in the history of Israel, as a fundamental fact. Only once that Angel, bent on slaying the firstborn; only once the slain lamb and sprinkled blood; only once the Exodus in the gray dawn of history. But the feast of the Passover, held in commemoration of that event, was destined to perpetual repetition until it gave place to a yet more significant symbol; which, in turn, is to fade into the marriage supper, as the love of betrothal fades into that of marriage, and moonlight into dawn.

The feast of Passover was held at Sinai; but not afterward till the forty years had lapsed. In fact, it could not be held while the nation, through unbelief and disobedience, was untrue to the covenant. Had it not been distinctly affirmed, amid other provisions, that no uncircumcised person should eat thereof? How, then, was it possible that it should be maintained, when, as we have lately learned, "all the people that were born in the wilderness, by the way as they came forth out of Egypt, they had not circumcized"? But as soon as the circumcising of the people was completed, there was no longer a barrier; and they kept the Passover between "the two evenings," as the sun of the fourteenth day of the month was flinging toward them long shadows from the palm trees and walls of Jericho.

There were two significant parts of the Passover as it was first instituted: the sprinkling of blood on the doors without; and within, the family gathered around the roasted lamb, and eating it in haste. As, however, years went on and conditions altered, blood was no longer sprinkled on the lintel and doorposts; but the drinking of wine was substituted for that ancient and significant act. And the family gathered round the table to the sacred feast, not merely with the girded loin and staff in hand as befitted pilgrims, but with the leisured restfulness of home. In point of fact, it was a family meal at which the people reviewed the past with thankfulness, and talked together of that mercy which had been so remarkably displayed in their national history. On reaching the Land of Promise, the thoughts of the people were guided back to the great fact of redemption by blood that lay at the basis of their existence. And there can never be a moment in the experience of the believer when he can be forgetful of the broken body and the shed blood of his Lord, broken and shed for the remission of sin. However much the cross may speak of santification, its primary message must ever be of justification. It is true that we died with him; but it is also true that he died for us—that he was made a curse to bring us blessings. In heaven itself the redeemed ones sing of the Lamb who was slain, and amid the raptures of the Golden City adore him who wrought redemption by his blood.

The other side of the Passover has also a counterpart in our experience. The Israelites feasted, they drank the light Eastern wine; and in after-days they chanted the Hallel, and ate of the flesh of the lamb. The bread was unleavened, and the herbs bitter; but joy preponderated over sorrow. And this is the type of Christian life. "Christ our Passover hath been sacrificed for us," said the apostle, "wherefore let us keep festival" (R.V.). He did not refer to any hour or day in the year when those to whom he wrote should give themselves up to joy. Instead he meant us to consider our lives as though the joy of the ancient Jewish feast is lengthened through all our days so that we are always standing with girded loins, always in the pilgrim attitude, and always feeding on the Lamb of God.

The Lord's Supper is not simply a memorial of what he did on Calvary, or is doing on the throne; it is a perpetual reminder to the believing heart of its privilege and duty to eat the flesh and drink the blood of the Son of Man after a spiritual sort. We must eat his flesh, or we shall have no life in us. We must drink his blood, or we shall not dwell in him, or he in us.

How little we understand the way by which each part of our body takes the particular nourishment it requires from the food we eat! But we know that such is the case; and that bones, muscles, and tissues appropriate their sustenance from the common store. So, though we may not be able to explain the philosophy of the process, we believe and are sure that as we hold fellowship with Jesus in quiet, hallowed moments, our weakness absorbs his strength, our impatience his long-suffering, our restlessness his calm, our ignorance his wisdom. But let it ever be borne in mind that as no uncircumcised person was permitted to partake of the Passover, so none who are living in willful sin can feed on the flesh and blood which were given for the life of the world. There must be a Gilgal before there can be a Passover in the deepest and fullest sense.

2. THE PRODUCE OF THE LAND. "And they did eat of the old corn of the land on the morrow after the Passover." There is no need for the adjective *old*. It would be sufficient to say that they ate of the corn of the land; though it is quite likely that it was the grain from the previous harvest, and not that which was then goldening throughout the land of Canaan, and ready for the sickle. The main point is that, with great thankfulness, the Israelites, the majority of whom had never tasted anything but manna, ate of the produce of the Land of Promise.

According to the Jewish code, on that day the high priest should have waved the first sheaf of the new harvest before God, so presenting the whole. The rite may have been omitted on that occasion, though religiously observed in later years. Is it not significant that on this very day the Lord Jesus arose from the dead, "the firstfruits of them that slept"? Surely, then, it is no straining of the parallel to say that the produce of the Land of Promise represents him in risen glory. He fell as a seed into the ground to die; but through death he has acquired the power of imparting himself to all who believe. He was bruised, as all grain for bread must be; the wheel of the cart of divine justice ground him beneath its weight. But he has become as a result the finest of the wheat to feed the needs of the world. We must feed on the Paschal Lamb, and learn the full meaning of his cross and passion, his precious death and burial; but we must also feed on the produce of the heavenly land, and derive life and blessing from his glorious resurrection and ascension.

The Church has in some measure learned to appreciate the importance of the incarnation and crucifixion. The picture galleries of the world teem with masterpieces representing the holy nativity and the wondrous cross. But it is comparatively seldom that we hear in treatise or sermon any adequate treatment of the ascension from the lowest parts of the earth to that zenith point of glory from which he fills all things. The resurrection is emphasized as the sign of his Sonship, and the evidence of his accepted work; but its full significance as the first step in the upward passage of the Son of God, bearing us with himself from glory to glory until we sat down with him in the heavenlies, is too little appreciated. Oh to know what Paul meant by his emphasis when he said, "*Yea rather*, that is risen again"; and to fathom his thought when he said that though he had known Christ after the flesh he wished to know him so no more, because he longed to understand the power of his resurrection. The Paschal Lamb is good; but the produce of the land includes the fruits and honey and breadstuff that grow on the soil of the resurrection life.

The ascension of Christ may be considered in many aspects; but in each we seem to stand beneath his out-stretched hands of benediction, as they did who saw him parted from them, and taken up before their adoring gaze. The majesty and triumph of the God-man, as he is raised far above all principality and power, whether of angels or of demons, and above every name that is named, whether in this world or that which is to come; the certainty that the same power which raised him from the grave to the right hand of the Father waits to do as much for each of us; the belief that in his ascension he has received gifts for each of us, and the best of all gifts, the fullness of the Spirit, waiting for us to claim and receive; the conception that, however our emotions may change, we are one with him, accepted and beloved—these are themes that stir our sluggish hearts and make them leap with gladness, which no increase of food or wine can yield to the men of this world. Happy indeed are they who also in heart and mind thither ascend, and *with him continually dwell.* To do this is to eat of the honey and fruit of the land.

3. THE MANNA. "And the manna ceased on the morrow, after they had eaten of the old corn of the land." There was no break between the two. The new provision began before the manna ceased. The one overlapped the other as the thatch of a haystack or the feathers of a bird.

God does not wish that there should be those intervals of apparent desertion and the failure of supplies of which so many complain. It is quite likely that he may have to withdraw the extraordinary and exceptional, as represented by the manna; but he will wait until we have become accustomed to the ordinary and regular supplies of his grace, as represented by the corn. In the blessings of our outward life he does sometimes humble us, and allow us to hunger. The brook Cherith dries before he sends us to Zarephath. But as to the inward life, he gives without stint. The table is always prepared before us in the presence of our enemies—one form of soul-sustenance is within reach before another form fails.

We are constantly being forced from the familiar manna which came without anxiety or seeking on our part, to the things which require foresight and careful preparation. This is needful; because in these we learn invaluable lessons of patience, and self-denial, and cooperation with God. But ah, how at first we shrink from the change! Who is there that does not cry, "The old is better"? The old furniture for the room; the old house where we spent so many happy days; the old familiar routine of life; the old ways of doing things. It is hard to part with them. But they have ceased to furnish the discipline we need; and we must leave them for the untried and unknown, where we obtain a new insight into the ways of God, and become workers together with him.

How gracious, then, is the gentle, thoughtful kindness of

God, who lets us see the new before he quite takes away the old; accustoming us to walk before he removes the chair on which we had leaned so long. Do not fret if the rhapsodies and outbursts and exuberant manifestations of earlier days have ceased; it is better to live by the ordinary laws of human life than by the abnormal and miraculous. And after all, there is as much divine power in the production of a fig and pomegranate, of olive oil and honey, of barley and wheat, as in the descending manna; as much in the transformation of the moisture of the earth and air into the ruddy grape as in the miracle of Cana; as much in the maintenance of the soul in holiness and righteousness all its days as in the communication of unspeakable visions and words that may not be uttered.

But in addition to all these lessons, we may learn from the cessation of the manna that, as we advance in Christian experience, we think less of the coming down from heaven in the incarnation and more of the going back in the ascension. The babe Jesus is less to us than the ascended Christ. We look not so much toward the cradle of the manger bed as upward to the throne and forward to the second advent. It makes a great difference to us whether we occupy the standpoint of the birth or of the ascension; and many a system of theology, when weighed in the balance, is found wanting because it fails to understand that the manna ceases when the Jordan is crossed and Canaan entered.

This, then, is our main lesson. We must learn to live in such a manner as to be nourished with the life of the Son of God. When we eat of Christ, we live by him, as he lived by the Father; and as the Father, dwelling in him, ministered through his life, and did his wondrous works, so he, entering into us—the Word by his words—will do through us what had otherwise been perfectly impossible.

Do you long for more strength to do or suffer, to witness or turn the foe from the gate? Then feed on Christ, meditating on his Word, communing with himself, filled by his Spirit, who takes of the things that are his and reveals them to us. "Blessed are they that hunger and thirst: they shall be filled." "He hath filled the hungry with good things." "Bread that strengtheneth man's heart."

7

THE WARRIOR CHRIST

(JOSHUA 5:13–15)

"So let it be. In God's own might
We gird us for the coming fight,
And, strong in him whose cause is ours
In conflict with unholy powers,
We grasp the weapons he has given—
The Light and Truth, and Love of Heaven."
WHITTIER

"I T came to pass." The time and exact locality are not defined; but they are not of much account in the presence of that marvelous episode which stands before the conquest of Canaan, as an illuminated capital before the black letterpress of some old missal. As to the time, it was probably the day in which the manna had ceased, and the Leader had realized that the land must now furnish the commissariat. As to the place, it is enough to know that it was *by Jericho*.

Behind lay the Jordan, the seam made by the passage of the host no longer discernible; though the fresh heap of memorial stones proclaimed the miracle of the dried riverbed. Beneath, under the shadow of the hill, lay the camp, where the people were resting from their long fatigues, in the first glad realization that their long journeyings were ended. While five miles distant, on the path to Canaan, towering above the palm groves, arose the strongly fortified walls of Jericho.

It must have been for Joshua, at least, a time of anxious suspense. He could not forget how forty years before the former generation had cried out for bondage in Egypt, or graves in the desert, rather than face the terrors of fortified cities and giant champions. And what might not their children do! It had been comparatively easy to cope with Amalek, and Og, and Sihon, because they had met Israel in open war upon the field of battle; but that was a very different matter to attacking a city which was able to hold its own in a long siege. It was impossible to leave it in the rear, unsubdued; but it was also suicidal to sit down before it to starve it to surrender. As the weary months dragged on, the energy of the people would evaporate, and the armies of their foes would gather. Eagerly must the lonely chieftain have longed for one moment with Moses, or, better still, with that Angel of the Presence of God, who had been promised when the camp was still pitched beneath the cliffs of Sinai.

Thinking much and deeply, Joshua wandered forth alone; and suddenly, "as he lifted up his eyes and looked, behold, there stood a man over against him, with his sword drawn in his hand." We need those uplifted eyes. Too often we keep our gaze fixed on the ground, and miss the celestial visions that await us all round.

But who was this man? Was he phantom or reality, Hebrew or Canaanite, friend or foe? Joshua knew not; but his heart was pure and clear, and therefore he did not hesitate to go up to him and challenge him with the inquiry, "Art thou for us, or for our adversaries?" Then came the majestic reply, "Nay; but as Captain of the host of the Lord am I now come." And Joshua fell on his face to the earth, and worshiped, and took the place of lowly obedience, saying, "What saith my Lord unto his servant?" We cannot doubt, then, who he was. Though bearing the semblance of a man, he was certainly neither man nor angel. Had he been either, he would have instantly repelled the homage which Joshua gave. When the men of Lystra were about to sacrifice to Paul and Barnabas, they cried out in horror, "Sirs, why do ye these things? We are men of like passions with you"; and when John, amid the blaze of glory, fell down before the feet of the angel who lifted the concealing veil, he said, "See thou do it not; for I am thy fellow-servant, and of thy brethren the prophets." But when Joshua prostrated himself before this mysterious apparition, there was no prohibition to his lowly homage. It was accepted as Peter's in the fishing boat; and as the leper's when he knelt at the blessed feet of Christ for healing. Joshua was even urged to more careful and reverent homage, in words which also were addressed to Moses from the burning bush, where the I AM spoke with him; and we have to believe that he who spoke to Joshua on the threshold of Canaan was none other than Jehovah, the God of Israel, whose delights, long before the incarnation, were with the sons of men, and who anticipated it by paying preliminary visits to our earth in corporeal form.

The title here adopted by our Lord clings to him throughout the Bible. Isaiah says that he is given to be the Leader and Commander of his people. Peter describes him as the Prince or Captain of Life. The Epistle to the Hebrews refers to him as the Captain of our Salvation, who was made perfect through suffering. And at the close of the Book we see a majestic procession come forth from the opened heaven, led by a Captain, who is clothed in vesture dipped in blood, and whose name is the Word of God.

1. THE SPECIAL SIGNIFICANCE OF THIS VISION TO JOSHUA. It has been generally supposed that this divine Captain came to take Joshua's place in command, and assume the supreme direction of the hosts of Israel; much as when the German Emperor takes the field, his

greatest officers subordinate themselves to him, surrendering to his hands the control of the campaign, and are content to execute his plans. But that is not the deepest meaning here. "The Lord's host" does not primarily allude to those Israelite armies encamped beside the overflowing waters of the Jordan; but to other and invisible hosts, encamped all around on those heights, though no ear ever heard the call of the sentries at their posts of duty, or saw the sheen of their swords flashing in the sunlight, or beheld their marshaled ranks. Those troops of harnessed angels were the hosts of which this wondrous warrior was Captain.

There are several references in Scripture to the presence, near at hand, of angel-hosts. When Jacob, after his angry altercation with Laban, was on his way back to Canaan, fearful perhaps of pursuit, we are told that the angels of God met him—as though a squadron of heavenly armies suddenly came in sight—assuring him of defense against attack. When the servant of the prophet was dismayed to find himself encircled by the hosts of Syria, he was permitted, in answer to Elisha's prayer, to see that the mountain was full of horses and chariots of fire. The Psalmist tells of the Angel that encamps around those who fear him, and of the hosts that do his bidding. So in Gethsemane, the Lord referred to the twelve legions of angels who were waiting, under arms, for the least indication of the Father's will—to come only too gladly to his relief. It is therefore in harmony with the tenor of Scripture to see those lines of warriors waiting within the curtains of the unseen to be led against the foes of God and Israel. And we read a new meaning into the ancient phrase by which Jehovah became known. "Who is the King of glory?" "The Lord of hosts, he is the King of glory."

But if it be true that there are hosts of light, it is certainly true also that there are hosts of darkness. Such is the perpetual affirmation of Scripture. Behind the gods of the heathen, inspiration detects demons, who rule men through the hideous idols of their hands. Behind the might of vast but ungodly empires inspired men descry the presence and activity of great potentates from Satan's fallen realm. Behind the darkness of this world the Bible teaches us to look for wicked spirits, who rule it from "the heavenlies." These they occupy for the present, and until the second advent hurls them down, first to the earth, and afterward to the abyss (1 Cor. 10:20; Dan.10:13; Eph. 6:12; Rev. 20:2-3).

Is it, therefore, any cause for wonder that the walls of Jericho fell down, or that vast armies were scattered without a blow being struck, or that the land was subdued in a seven-year campaign? These achievements were the earthly and visible results of victories won in the heavenly and spiritual sphere by armies which follow the Word of God upon white horses, clothed in fine linen, white and pure. Those walls fell down because smitten by the impact of celestial hosts. Those armies fled because the dark powers with which they were in league had been put to the rout before the Lord God of Sabaoth. That land was subdued because of some great dislodgment which had taken place in regions beyond human ken. There was therefore deep significance in the words with which Caleb had sought to encourage his people forty years before: "Their defense is removed from over them, and the Lord is with us: fear them not." And we can better understand what the Lord meant when he said, "As Captain of the Lord's host am I now come."

2. THE SIGNIFICANCE OF THIS VISION TO THE CHURCH. If we read the thoughts thus suggested into the story of the conquest of Canaan, we shall find it invested with fresh interest. It is, as we have said, not only an ancient historic record, but a page torn out of the chronicles of heaven, telling of that mighty conflict which has been in process since the introduction of moral evil, and shall last till the Son of God has destroyed the works of the devil.

Throughout the world of nature there are signs of conflict and collision. Everywhere armies meet in battleshock, and part to repair their losses or count their gains. According to the last findings of science, the invisible molecules of the calmest air are in rapid motion all around us, jostling with each other, and fighting hard to keep their course, but hindered by a thousand kindred molecules that are fighting too, so that we move and work in a very cyclone of whirling atoms. There is no pool, however tranquil; no forest glade, however peaceful; no isle bathed by southern seas, and set gem-like on the breast of ocean, however enchanting; no scene, however fascinating—which is not swept by opposing squadrons contending for victory. The swift pursue their prey; the strong devour the weak; the fittest alone survive in the terrific strife.

For the student of God's ways all this leads up to a more tremendous struggle, between darkness and light, evil and good, Satan and our King. And here is the real importance of the ascension, which was the worthy climax of the wonders of the first advent, as it will introduce the glories of the second.

All through his earthly ministry our Lord encountered the dark powers. They assailed him in the wilderness of temptation; opposed him through the wretched victims they possessed; gathered in their might in the glades of Gethsemane; hissed their horrid suggestions into his heart on the cross; and resisted his every step as he arose. Up to that moment none of woman born had proved himself able to overcome their attacks. But the life and death of the man Christ Jesus turned the tide. And when he arose and ascended far above all rule and authority and power and dominion and every name that is named, not only in this world but also in that which is to come, it became established beyond a doubt that though man in himself was no match for hell, yet man in Christ, in union with the Son of God, was more than a conqueror; able to do all things through him that strengthened him, and destined to overcome.

The victory of the ascension was not for Jesus only, but for his people; that he might lead his heavenly squadrons forth to assured victory, while the Church militant marched on the plains of earth below. When the Church won her mightiest victories over the idols of Greece and Rome, the systems of pagan philosophy, the temples of Venus and Diana and Jove, she recognized this; and her successes were due, not to the valor or prowess of her battalions, but to the spiritual forces with which she was allied. To this same cause, whether recognized or not, we must attribute the missionary triumphs of recent years—the open doors; the tottering of heathen systems; the unopposed progress of the gospel in many lands. These results have been doubtless simultaneous with changes in the sphere of the Unseen and Eternal, of which we can form no true conception; and the future conquests of the Church must depend, not on her wealth or numbers or prestige, but on her loving and hallowed alliance with those celestial hosts to which the Lord Jesus referred on the plains of Jericho when he said, "As Captain of the Lord's host am I now come."

Alas, that this truth has been so little appreciated! The Church of Christ has too often either considered that she contained within herself all the resources necessary for victory over the evil of the world, or she has stood paralyzed or aghast before the Jerichos of sin which have risen up to obstruct her path. The fenced cities of drink and lust, of self-indulgence or apathy, have refused to open their gates to her challenge, and have laughed defiance to her hosts. Then she has appealed to Caesar—to human methods and alliances and expedients. But in vain; for notwithstanding all, the walls have not fallen down, nor her foes given back.

The saints of God have need to repent of their sins and failures in this direction. Let them realize that already the Captain of the celestial hosts has led his squadrons against their foes and his. Let them put away all that would imperil or impair the alliance. Let them raise a modification of the old battle cry, which was originally based on an acknowledgment of this great spiritual fact, and charge with the shout, "The sword of the Lord and of his people."

3. THE SIGNIFICANCE OF THIS VISION TO OURSELVES. We sometimes feel lonely and discouraged. The hosts with which we are accustomed to cooperate are resting quietly in their tents. No one seems able to enter into our anxieties and plans. Our Jerichos are so formidable—the neglected parish; the empty church; the hardened congregation; the godless household. How can we ever capture these, and hand them over to the Lord, like dismantled castles, for him to occupy?

That problem at first baffles us, and appears insoluble. Then we vow it shall be untied, and summon all our wit and energy to solve it. We study the methods of others, and copy them; deliver our best addresses and sermons; put forth herculean exertions; we adopt exciting advertisements and questionable methods, borrowed from the world. Suppose Israel had taken lessons in scaling walls and taking fenced cities from the Canaanites! Or that the people had made an attack on Jericho with might and main, determined to find or make a breach! Such suppositions are not altogether absurd. At least they have their counterpart in the practice of too many of God's children, who forget that the race is not to the swift, nor the battle to the strong, and that by strength shall no man prevail.

But in our hours of disappointment, when we have tried our best in vain, and have fallen—as the sea birds which dash themselves against the lighthouse tower fall to the foot with broken wing—it is well to go forth alone, confessing our helplessness, and tarrying for the vision; for then we shall be likeliest to see the Captain of the

Lord's host. He will undertake our cause; he will marshal his troops and win the day; he will fling the walls of Jericho to the ground. Those walls can only fall down by faith; for faith allies itself with omnipotence, and becomes the channel along which the might of God can pass, as the electric current along the wire. Our cooperation may be employed, but only to walk around the walls, in the garb of priestly purity, and blowing the rams' horns.

But we must be holy. "Put off thy shoes from off thy feet," said the divine Warrior to Joshua; "for the place whereon thou standest is holy." Wherever God is, there is holiness. Even Canaan is holy when God stands upon its soil. And we must be holy if we would cooperate with him. We must put off the old man, with his affections and lusts; we must cleanse ourselves from all filthiness of the flesh and spirit; we must cast off the works of darkness, and array ourselves in the panoply of light.

We know enough to be sure that he will not ally himself with the unfaithful or unclean, or have any association with us so long as we harbor an Achan with wedge of gold and Babylonish garment. And if he is to go forth with our armies, to deliver us and to give up our enemies before us, we must be careful that the camp be holy, and that he see no unclean thing in us and turn away (Deut. 23:14).

The battle is not to the strong, nor the race to the swift; but each to those who are living lives separate from the world, and dedicated to God. The vessels which are fit for the Master's use are pure ones. Cleanness, rather than cleverness, is the prime condition of successful service. And then it is only out of such a heart that the faith can spring which is able to wield the forces of the unseen and spiritual and divine. May there be no film between God's holiness and ours! Nothing to insulate us or shut off the current! No shoe leather to intercept the communication of its fullness to our need.

8

THE WALLS OF JERICHO

(JOSHUA 6)

"More than conquerors even now,
With the war-sweat on our brow,
Onward o'er the well-marked road,
March we as the host of God."
H. BONAR

JERICHO, palm-girt, standing out clear-cut in the pure air and under the deep blue of the sky, in front of the vast precipice of rock down which the road descended from Jerusalem, was filled with many thoughts, chief among which was faint-heartedness. There was no mustering of forces; no issuing forth of the men of war; no sudden night attack upon that host which lay along the Jordan bank, the brown tents pitched around the central pavilion or tabernacle of God. It was as though some mysterious spell had fallen upon king and people, unnerving them, impelling them to remain upon the defensive and await the unfolding of events. "Their heart melted, neither was there spirit in them any more, because of the children of Israel."

Israel, on the other hand, was probably impatient, eager to be led to the conflict. The men of war, confident in their might, were eager to match themselves against the inhabitants of the land, and to wipe out in blood the memory of their fathers' defeat at Hormah. Conscious that the passage of the Jordan had been due to the presence of the priests, it may have been that there was a secret desire in their hearts to show that the time had come for the priests to stand aside, while they demonstrated their powers and won the land by might.

But they had to learn that the land was a gift, to be received by faith, not won by effort. God required of them only to obey and wait and trust, while the divine Captain led his celestial hosts to the assault, and achieved the victory. "And the Lord said unto Joshua, See, I have given into thine hand Jericho, and the king thereof, and the mighty men of valor. And ye shall compass the city, all the men of war, going about the city once" (R.V.).

It certainly was the strangest spectacle ever witnessed by a beleaguered garrison. The besiegers did not make an assault, or rear mounds, or place scaling-ladders against the walls. Nor did they offer an opportunity for parley or discussion of terms of capitulation. On each side it seems to have been understood that the war would be to the knife—no quarter asked, no mercy shown. Without delay the army of Israel began to march around the city. "Ye shall compass the city." May it not be rather said that *the ark* went around the city, and that the men of war accompanied it? For in each case, whether the directions were given to Joshua by the Captain, or by Joshua to the army, the particular position of the ark was minutely specified. Indeed, as Joshua came from the divine interview he appears to have first summoned the priests into his presence, and given them his instructions. After this, he turned to the people generally. There is a remarkable emphasis in the words, "He caused the ark of the Lord to compass the city."

It was but a little after dawn. The sun had mounted not far above the eastern horizon. Blue blended with amber

IN THE DEFEAT AT HORMAH, NEITHER THE ARK OR MOSES LEFT THE CAMP.

in the morning sky. Toward the south the mountains of Moab stood like a mighty rampart, veiled in violet, while the sullen waters of the Dead Sea gleamed like silver at their foot. The belt of desert sand added its dark red to the variegated colors of the picture, contrasting notably with the emerald green of the oasis in which Jericho stood, watered by perennial streams. Then from out the camp of Israel a long procession began to unwind itself: first the men of war, marching beneath their tribal banners; then seven priests, white-robed, blowing with seven trumpets of rams' horns; next the ark of God, hidden by its coverings from gaze of Israelite and Canaanite alike; and a rear guard at the end.

Toward the city this strange procession made its way, preserving an absolute silence, except that the priests went on continually and blew with the trumpets. With that exception no other sound was heard. No challenge! No taunt! No cry as of those who shout for mastery! The whole host wound silently around the city, as a serpent with sinuous folds; and when the circuit was completed, to the surprise of the Canaanites, who probably expected an immediate assault, it returned quietly to the camp from which it had emerged an hour or two before. And the rest of the day passed without further incident. "So they did six days."

On the seventh day the circuit of the walls was repeated seven times. And at the close of the seventh, Joshua's voice rang out on the still evening air the command, "Shout; for the Lord hath given you the city." Then the priests blew a blast upon the trumpets; the people shouted with a great shout, that reverberated through the hills around, and was perhaps answered by the feebler voices of the women and children from the camp; and the wall of Jericho fell down flat, so that the people could go up into the city, every man straight before him, "and they took the city." As, in years long after, an inspired writer reviewed the incident, he quoted it as a remarkable instance of that faith which, in various dispensations, unites the hearts of all the saints in one, as a thread links a number of diverse beads. "By faith the walls of Jericho fell down, after they had been compassed about for seven days" (Heb. 11:30, R.V.). In various directions we may find a counterpart of this remarkable incident:

1. IN CHRISTIAN EXPERIENCE. If Egypt represents our conflicts with the world, and Amalek our conflict with the flesh, the seven nations of Canaan represent our conflict with the principalities and powers of wicked spirits, who resist our entrance into the heavenlies, and dull our practical realization of what Christ has accomplished for us. Intrenched behind the ramparts of some stronghold of difficulty or habit, they defy us and threaten to arrest our progress in the divine life. Who is there among us, or who reads these lines, that does not know, or has not known, of something—a cherished indulgence, a friendship, a pernicious entanglement—reared as an impassable barrier to the enjoyment of those blessed possibilities of Christian experience which are ours in Christ, but which for that reason seem beyond our reach? That thing is a Jericho.

Now it cannot be the purpose of God that anything, however deeply rooted, should shut his redeemed ones out of the heavenly places, which are theirs in Christ—even though it should be the result of their own sin or mistake, the heirloom of early indiscretions, the bitter aftermath of trespass off the narrow path. I have met with those who have declared that they have forever forfeited their right to the richer experiences of the blessed life because they have wrought some wickedness in the past. Even though it has long ago been forgiven, yet it has left its shame, its scar, its fatal offspring, by reason of which, in their apprehension, their path into Canaan is barred. I have met with others who, eager enough to enjoy all that may be experienced on this side the Golden Gate, yet point to some hindrance in the way, the lasting memorial of days when the spirit was less on the alert, and conscience less sensitive; and for this cause they too fear that they can never do more than encamp, across the Jordan indeed, but on the fringe of the Land of Promise. But again I must ask, who is there that has not stood, at some period or another, before a Jericho, right in the pass to Canaan?

To all such there is infinite sweetness and comfort in the word spoken by the Great Captain to Joshua, standing with bared foot on the holy ground, "See, I have given into thine hand Jericho, and the king thereof, and the mighty men of valor."

Be still! The hardest of all commandments is this. That our voice should not be heard; that no word should proceed from our mouth; that we should utter our complaints to God alone—all this is foreign to our habits and taste. As death is the last enemy to be destroyed in the universe of God, so is the restraint of the tongue the last lesson learned by his children. We like to air our grievances; to talk over our ailments; to compare ourselves with others; and to discuss the likeliest remedies. We tell our friends our secrets under strict promises of confidence, to discover in bitter experience the truth of the Master's words, that what is told into the ear in closets will be proclaimed upon housetops.

It is only the still heart that can reflect the heaven of God's overarching care, or detect the least whisper of his voice through its quiet atmosphere, or know his full grace and power. Only when we have quieted ourselves as weaned babes can we reach that position in which God can interpose for our help. Not silent toward God, but silent as the dove among strangers, or as the lamb before her shearers. "Be still," says God, "and know that I am God. I will be exalted among the heathen; I will be exalted in the earth." And that soul may well be still and wait which has learned that the Lord of hosts is beside it and the God of Jacob its refuge. To that Friend it rushes to pour out its secret agony. In that home it nestles as in the covert of a great rock, sheltered from the blast.

Obey! As in this story so in grace, there must be cooperation between God and man. The walls of Jericho could fall down only by the exercise of divine power; but the children of Israel must needs encompass them. Only God can give a body as it has pleased him to the seed; but man must plow and sow and reap and thresh and grind. Only the Son of God could multiply the loaves or raise the dead; but man must provide and distribute the broken bread, and roll the stone from the sepulcher door. Only God can remove the difficulties that stand in the way of an entirely consecrated and blessed life; but there are commands and duties which it is incumbent on us to fulfill.

What are these? In some cases we are withholding obedience that we should give at once. There are things which we ought to do, but which we are not doing. And there is equal danger in doing more than we should— endeavoring to scale walls which we are told to march around; shouting before the word of command has been uttered; making the circuit of the city oftener than the once each day prescribed by the divine ordering. It is so hard to feel that we do more by doing less; that we save time by resting quietly in our tents; that it is vain to rise up early, and so late take rest, because he gives to his beloved while they sleep.

Whatever, then, is clearly borne in on us as the will of God, either for us to do or discontinue doing, let us immediately perform; and leave it to him to do all the rest. Some must bear the sacred ark in witnessing to the gospel; others must blow on the rams' horns perpetual blasts of victorious anticipation; others, again, must face the daily routine in silence. But our position should ever be the prompt soldier-like one that rang out through Joshua's noble words: "What saith my Lord unto his servant?"

Have faith! Look away from all your preparations, and even from your God-commanded acts to God himself; and as you do so, your difficulties will melt away. That stone will be rolled from the mouth of the sepulcher; that iron gate will open of its own accord; those mighty walls will fall down flat.

Whatever it be that seems an insuperable difficulty to your enjoyment of the best of those things which Christ has purchased, hand it over to your Saviour; wait before him in silence, till you know what he would have you do. Be sure in the meanwhile to put off all that belongs to the past, and cleanse yourself from all filthiness of the flesh and spirit; then do his bidding, at whatever cost. At the same time believe that he is working for you, and that the crooked places shall be made straight, and the rough places smooth, and that the glory of the Lord shall be seen in your heart and life, so that all who know you shall be compelled to confess that the Lord has done great things for you. He has given you Jericho. Let your heart already dwell on that glad word. Though the walls are yet standing, they are as good as gone; and with their ruins in your rear, you shall go forward to possess the land.

2. IN CHRISTIAN WORK. The apostle speaks of strongholds that had to be cast down, and of high things that exalted themselves against the knowledge of God; and asserts that he did not war against such things according to the flesh, and that the weapons of his warfare were not of the flesh, but mighty before God for the casting down of strongholds, and for the bringing of every high and proud thought into captivity to the obedience of Christ.

What need there is for all Christian workers to ponder these pregnant words! The peril of our time is that we should get away from the simplicity of the early Church, which went into the conflict against the mighty superstitions and flagrant sins of its age with no weapons except those that may be found in symbol in this old-world incident. There were the white robes of priestly purity—the lifting up of the propitiation of Christ; the blowing of the rams' horns—the gospel message proclaimed with no silver cadence, but with rude and startling effect, as a summons to surrender. It was in the use of such weapons as these that giant forms of error collapsed, and hoary systems of idolatry were dissolved like morning mists touched by the warm fingers of the sun.

With what dismay would the confessors and martyrs, the prophets and apostles of primitive Christianity view the methods with which we assail the monster forms of vice that confront us! Drink is intrenched behind mighty fortifications—the bastions and walls of social custom and habit, of national usage and immense revenues. Impurity has built around itself a girdle of defense, flaunts itself undismayed in our streets, and mocks us from the gilded splendor of music hall and theater. The opium traffic laughs us to scorn—supported by government; ministering to an inveterate habit; willing to pay a handsome sum for its right to exist. The depravity of the human heart is another Jericho, in which there are the towers of spiritualism, indifference, pride, and high imagination, which proudly rear themselves against the law of God. And in the case of each individual worker there is almost certainly some Jericho in the apathy of fellow-workers, the spirit of opposition from other Christians, or the special forms of sin that are rampant in the sphere entrusted to his care.

When confronted with all these things we are apt to fight the world with weapons borrowed from its arsenals, and to adopt methods which savor rather of the flesh than of the spirit. It is a great mistake. Our only hope is to act on strictly spiritual lines, because we wrestle not with flesh and blood, but with the wicked spirits that lie behind all that is seen in this world of men and things. If we can overthrow the dark spirits that abet and maintain, we shall see the system which they support crumble as a palace of clouds before the wind.

Let us be pure and holy, giving time to heart searching in the presence of the Captain; let us lift up the sacrifice and work of Jesus; let us blow the gospel trumpet of alarm and summons to surrender; let us be much in silent prayer before God; let us cherish a spirit of unity and love, as the tribes of Israel forgot their differences in one common expedition against their foes; above all, let us believe in the presence and cooperation of God, and we shall see the old miracle repeated, and the walls of Jericho fall down flat.

3. IN THE STORY OF THE CHURCH. This capture of Jericho is surely capable of being read as a parable of things that are yet to be. We know that the world lies in the power of the wicked one. It has long boasted itself against God, with its mighty walls and gates; and it would seem as if the time will never come of which psalmists and kings have sung and spoken in rapturous phrase.

In the meanwhile the various tribes of the Church of Christ have been perambulating about the walls, subjected to much derision and mockery, though sometimes a sickening premonition of approaching judgment must steal upon the hearts of the votaries of worldliness. For nearly nineteen centuries the circuit has been made, the trumpet blast uttered, the testimony maintained. And surely the seven days have nearly expired.

It may be that this narrative of the taking of Canaan is even a miniature anticipation of what is yet to transpire in that future which is probably so near. God has given the kingdoms of this world to his Son; but they will have to be engirdled by the sacramental hosts of his elect until he shall have put down all rule and authority and power.

9

ARREST AND DEFEAT

(JOSHUA 7:1–13)

"Now, Christians, hold your own—the land before ye
Is open—win your way, and take your rest.'
So sounds our war-note; but our path of glory
By many a cloud is darkened and unblest."
KEBLE

T HE conquest of Canaan occupied seven years, and during the whole of that time Israel lost but one battle; indeed, the thirty-six men smitten in the headlong flight before the men of Ai seem to have been the only loss which their hosts sustained. The story of this defeat is told with great minuteness, because it involved lessons of the greatest importance to Israel, and of incalculable value to ourselves.

The experience of defeat is far too common to the majority of Christians. They are constantly turning their backs before their enemies. They are defeated by indwelling sin and the assaults of Satan, and by the mighty evils which they assail in the name of God. But instead of taking their defeats to heart, they become inured to them. For the time they are filled with mortification and chagrin, but the impression soon wears away. They do not lie on their faces before God, eager to discover the cause of failure, to deal with it, and to advance from the scene of defeat to wider and more permanent success. If we but carefully investigated the causes of our defeats, they would be only second to victories in their blessed results on our character and lives.

There were three causes for this defeat:

1. THEY WERE SELF-CONFIDENT BECAUSE AI WAS SMALL. Jericho was a heap of smoldering ruins. Man and woman, both young and old, and ox and sheep and ass, all had been utterly destroyed with the edge of the sword. The only relics were the silver and gold and vessels of brass and iron which had been placed among the precious stores of the Tabernacle; the woman Rahab, her people and her property; and a certain Babylonish garment, some silver shekels, and a wedge of gold, of which we shall hear again.

Fearing no attack from the rear, Joshua at once set his face toward the interior of the country, and chose a deep gorge or ravine, which lay a little toward the north, as the passageway for his army. Eight miles from its opening on the Jordan valley this ravine met another, "in a wild entanglement of hill and valley," and near the junction of the two stood the little town of Ai, with a population of twelve thousand persons. The proportion of fighting men has been calculated at about two thousand; but the situation was strong and commanded the pass, so that Joshua had no alternative but to mete out to it the same terrible fate as that which he had visited upon Jericho.

Speaking after the manner of men, there was considerable persuasion in the report of the spies sent up the valley to reconnoiter. The place was much smaller than Jericho, and would apparently require much less expenditure of time and strength for its capture. Jericho may have needed the entire army; but for Ai, some three thousand men would surely suffice. "Make not all the people to toil thither; for they [the men of Ai] are but few."

But this recommendation went on the supposition that Jericho had been overthrown by the attack of the hosts of Israel; whereas, in point of fact, they had had singularly little to do with it. They had walked around it, and shouted—that was all. It had been taken by their great Captain and Leader, and by him given into their hands. The silence that reigned over its site was no criterion of their might, but of his. To speak as they did was to ignore the real facts of the case, and to argue as though the victory were due to some inherent qualities in themselves, with the inference that because they had conquered at Jericho they must therefore necessarily conquer at Ai.

There is no experience in the Christian life so full of peril as the hour when we are flushed with recent victory. Then comes the temptation to sacrifice to our net, and burn incense to our dragnet (Hab. 1:16). We magnify our part in the conflict till it fills the whole range of vision. We boast to ourselves that we have gotten the land in possession by our own sword, and that our own arm has saved us. Counting from our great triumph at Jericho, we despise such a small obstacle as Ai. Surely, we argue, if we have carried the one, we shall easily prevail at the other! And so it frequently happens that a great success in public is followed by a fall in private; that those who had swept all before them in the pulpit or on the platform are overcome by some miserable appetite, or by petulance in the home; and the bitter regret of that sin wipes out all the glad exhilaration of the hour of victory. We never so need to observe the injunction to "watch and pray" as when the foe is fleeing before us. When the mighty convocation breaks up, its convictions having been turned by our single voice—as in the story of Elijah— and as the people are departing to their homes and the bodies of the priests of Baal choke the Kishon, we must be careful to go up to the top of Carmel, where we had girded ourselves for the conflict, and, bowing to the earth, put our face between our knees in prayer.

Had Joshua acted thus, he would never have been induced by the words of the spies to reason on mere military grounds; he would never have presumed on the insignificance of the little town; and he would never have had the anguish of seeing his panic-stricken soldiers come rushing down the rugged pass, or sheltering in the stone quarries on either hand, while the men of Ai, in full pursuit, were cutting down the hindmost and least nimble.

There is nothing small in the Christian life—nothing so small that we can combat it in our own strength. Apart from God, the smallest temptations will be more than a match for us. So weak are we that occasions of sin, which are perfectly contemptible in themselves, will overthrow our most confident resolutions. The victories which we have won in fellowship with God have imparted no inherent might to us; we are as weak as ever; and as soon as we are brought into collision with the least of our enemies, apart from him, we shall inevitably go down before the shock. The faith, watchfulness, and fellowship with God, which availed before Jericho, can alone serve as the key to Ai.

2. THEY FAILED TO WAIT ON GOD. An accursed thing in their midst broke the link of fellowship between them and the hosts that served beneath the celestial Warrior who had appeared to Joshua. And though it must have been a severe sorrow to Jehovah to inflict sorrow on his people, yet for their sake, and for the sake of his holy name, the sin must be judged and put away. Joshua pleaded, "What wilt thou do for thy great name?" But it was for that very reason that the defeat had been permitted.

There is not the least doubt that if Joshua had been in abiding fellowship with God, the Spirit of God would have indicated the presence of evil in the host; so that

Achan and his sin would have been discovered and judged before the march to Ai. It was so in an analogous case in the Acts of the Apostles. What Achan was to Israel, that Ananias and his wife were to the early Church. The fifth chapter of the Acts would have recorded some great defeat or crushing disaster if it had not contained the account of the discernment on the part of the Apostle Peter, and by the Holy Spirit, of the accursed thing to which the guilty pair were privy.

If we may dare to imagine what would have been the consequence in the primitive Church had that root of evil been left unextirpated, we should be obliged not only to wipe out the record of the signs and wonders wrought among the people, of the unity of the disciples, and of the burst doors of the prison; but we should have to interpolate an account of how the people of God, in diminished numbers, retreated before the fury of their adversaries; of how Peter lay with his face in the dust of the Temple courts; of how panic and dismay filled the hearts of both the leaders and the led; and of how the name of the Lord Jesus was blasphemed, and his character traduced. But none of these things occurred, because the Spirit of God was able to utter his unhindered testimony.

Very important is it for us to heed the apostle's warning, "If we discerned ourselves we should not be judged" (1 Cor. 11:31, R.V.). God sees the little rift in the lute; the spot of decay in the fruit; the ulcer in the flesh, threatening to eat away its vitality. These may not be realized by us; but he knows how inevitably they must lead to defeat. Nor is he slow to warn us of them. Yet of what use is it for him to speak to deaf ears; or to those who are self-confident in their own wisdom; or who pride themselves on victories which were wholly his gift? Amid the gaiety of the revel, we do not see the handwriting on the wall; amid the unanimous advice of the false prophets, we do not inquire for the one voice that may speak evil of our plans; amid the radiant sunlight of the morning, in which the dancing wavelets flash, we do not care to see the falling barometer, or be guided by the dark prognostications of the weather-beaten sailor. Probably there is no single temptation which has not to claim permission of God before it touches us. He who permits it prays for us, raising his voice in lonely vigil while we sleep, anticipating the attack by ambushes of intercession (Rom. 8:26–27). Yea, not content with this, he warns us not once or twice; he even touches us with fingers that would thrill us were we not insensible, steeped in spiritual lethargy.

Where God's children, like Joshua, are oblivious to the warning voices which speak in ever fainter tones as they are disregarded, God is compelled to let them take their course until some terrible disaster flings them on their faces to the ground. Ah, if Joshua had only prostrated himself amid the shoutings of victory over Jericho, there would have been no need for him to prostrate himself amid the outcry of a panic-stricken host! If he had only sought counsel of God before he sent the spies up the pass, there would have been no need to ask what he should do to repair his defeat. The iron pruning-knife of trouble has to do for many of us, roughly and hurtfully, what the silver pruning-knife of the Word of God might have effected.

Before we make any new advance, although the point of attack be but an Ai, it is our duty, as it is our best policy, to get back to Gilgal. Joshua does not seem to have returned there after the fall of Jericho. We ought to seclude ourselves in spiritual dialogue with our Almighty Ally, asking if he has anything to say to us; entreating that he would reveal any evil thing that he may see in us, and mustering the tribes of our heart before his scrutiny, that the Achan lurking there may be brought to light before, instead of after, the fight.

3. THEY HAD COMMITTED A TRESPASS IN THE DEVOTED THING.

(a) Joshua was inclined to lay the charge of their failure on God. It seemed to him as if the Almighty had done ill by them in bringing them into the heart of such mighty difficulties. In his judgment, warped by the presence of disaster, it appeared as if it had been better for the camp to have remained on the other side of Jordan. The dreariest anticipations of defeat and destruction passed in spectral form before him. He spoke as one whom faith had deserted, the locks of his might shorn, and himself no longer a hero, but, like the Canaanites themselves, whose heart had melted as his did now. But, in point of fact, the blame lay not with God, who was engaged in conducting his people within reach of superlative blessedness, but wholly with themselves.

There are times in our lives when we are disposed to find fault with God. "Why, Great Potter, have you made me as I am? Why was I ever taken out of my quiet home, or country parish, or happy niche of service, to be plunged into this sea of difficulties?" When we are smarting from some defeat, caused by the overpowering might or the clever strategy of the foe, we are prone to blame God; either that our nature was not stronger, or that he has brought us from the shelter of comparative obscurity and placed us on the mountain slope where the storms expend their wildest fury. Alas! We forget that our Father brings us across the Jordan to give us larger experiences, to open before us vaster possibilities, to give us a better chance of acquiring his unsearchable riches. There is no task without sufficiency of grace; no foe without a sufficiency of victorious power; no trial without a sufficiency of resource by which, as in the old dream of the alchemist, the hardest, commonest metal may be transformed to gold.

The defeats that we incur in the Land of Promise are not necessary. They are due entirely to some failure in ourselves, and they cause grief to the immortal Lover of our souls. There is no reason for defeat in the Christian life; always and everywhere we are meant to be more than conquerors. The course of the Christian warrior should be as the sun when he goeth forth in his strength, and in regular gradients drives his chariot from the eastern wave up the steep of heaven. Child of God, never lay the blame of your failure on God; seek for it within!

(b) One Israelite only had trespassed, and yet it is said, "*The children of Israel* committed a trespass in the devoted thing." Not one of us stands alone; we cannot sin without insensibly affecting the spiritual condition of all our fellows. We cannot grow cold without lowering the temperature of all contiguous hearts. We cannot pass upward without lifting others. No asteroid revolves through space without affecting the position and speed of every member of its system. No grain of sand lies upon the seashore without influencing all its companion grains. "None of us liveth to himself, and none dieth to himself." "Whether one member suffereth, all the members suffer with it; or one member is honored, all the members rejoice with it."

If Israel had but realized how much the safety of the whole depended on the obedience of each, every individual would have watched his brethren as he watched himself, not for their sakes alone but for his own; and did the members of Christian communities understand how vast an influence for weal or woe depends upon the choice, the decision, the action of any, there would be a fuller and more intelligent obedience to the reiterated injunctions of the New Testament—for the strong to bear the infirmities of the weak; for the loftiest to stoop to wash the feet of the lowliest; and for all to look not on their own things only, but also on the things of others. "Looking carefully lest any man fail of the grace of God."

Should these words be read by any soul which is conscious of playing an Achan's part, let it take warning, and while it is called today, confess, restore, and repent. Not only that it may escape an inevitable judgment; but that it may not bring disaster and defeat upon those with whom it associates, dragging the innocent down into the vortex of a common fate. The hands of Achan were stained with the blood of the thirty-six that perished in the flight to Shebarim.

(c) How careless we are of God's distinct prohibitions! Nothing could have been more clearly promulgated than the command to leave the spoils of Jericho untouched. The city and its contents were devoted to utter destruction, a specified number of articles only being preserved for Tabernacle use. This ordinance was probably intended to protect the children of Israel from the temptation which must have accrued had they glutted themselves with the spoils of the city. The abstinence tended to strengthen their character, and to educate their faith. But to Achan, the will of God was overborne by the lust of his eyes and the pride of life. The strong tide of passion swept him over the barrier reared by the divine word.

Let us not, however, judge him too harshly. He is not the last who has acted in distinct violation of divine commands. The Bible is full of prohibitions against the love of the world, the love of dress, the love of money; against censoriousness, and pride, and unhallowed ambition; against the Babylonish garment and the wedge of gold. And yet thousands of Christian people live in complacent disobedience, as if God were one of themselves, or as if his words were as unsubstantial as smoke. What wonder that the forces of his Israel meet with defeat, and that the old word is verified in individual experience and in the history of the Church: "Israel hath sinned; yea, they have even transgressed my covenant which I commanded them; yea, they have even taken of the devoted thing. Therefore they cannot stand before their enemies. I will not be with you any more, except ye destroy the devoted thing from among you" (R.V.).

10

THE VALLEY OF ACHOR

(JOSHUA 7:14–8:28)

"No cloud across the sun
But passes at the last, and gives us back
The face of God once more."
KINGSLEY

W AS it a sudden gust of temptation that swept Achan before it when, with the rest of the army, he entered Jericho? Or was it that some long growth of unjudged evil flowered into that act which has made his name a reproach to all who go after? It is impossible to say. Only the terribleness of his fate seems to indicate something more than a transient yielding to sin. This, at least, is clear, that in the late afternoon of the day of Jericho's capture, and before the lurid flames of its conflagration rose to heaven, he had pilfered one of those robes of exquisite texture for which the plain of Shinar was famous, together with gold and silver—the latter coined, the former in a wedge—and had borne them surreptitiously away.

We can imagine him bringing them into his tent, where he probably found it necessary to acquaint his children with his deed; for if they had not been party to the crime and its concealment, they could hardly have been involved in his terrible fate. With their help he dug a hole in the sand and hid the spoil, which by the special ban of Joshua had been devoted to Jehovah.

The whole proceeding had been conducted in such absolute secrecy, and he was so confident of the collusion of the inmates of his tent, that, amid the general inquiry for the thief, he braved detection, and held his peace until the unerring finger of God pointed him out, as if he had said, "Thou art the man!"

But what anguish he must have suffered in the meanwhile! Long before his deed was unmasked, conscience had borne witness against him; and the lot had been cast within the circle of his heart. The scene in which he played so prominent a part on the plains of Jericho was rehearsed where no crowds of awestruck spectators gathered round, no blanched faces looked upon his, and no horror-stricken messengers ran to the tent to unearth the hidden treasure.

When the first excitement of his new acquisition had passed, and the fever had subsided, the dull, heavy sense of wrongdoing began to gnaw at his heart. In the lull of reaction, conscience spoke; and when he marched with the rest up the long ravine to Ai, when he saw his comrades turn to flee, when he joined in the breathless rush back to the camp, when he met the relatives of the thirty-six men who had fallen in the battle, when he saw the dismay beneath which Joshua and the elders of Israel were overwhelmed—he knew, by an unerring spiritual perception, that it was his sin that was bringing shame and disaster to Israel. It must have been a positive relief to him when his secret was torn from his breast, and there was no need to preserve longer the appearance of comparative unconcern. Let us turn aside and study this scene in which Achan's sin was detected and dealt with; for while we do so, we may learn something of the action of that sharp, two-edged sword which pierces to the dividing asunder of soul and spirit, and discerns the thoughts and intents of the heart.

1. WE SHOULD GRIEVE MORE FOR SIN THAN FOR ITS RESULTS. Joshua rent his clothes, and fell to the earth upon his face before the ark of the Lord until the evening, smarting from the disgrace inflicted upon his people, and aghast at the results which would probably ensue as soon as the tidings had been voiced abroad. Judging simply by human standards, the very worst consequences might be expected when the nations of Canaan suddenly discovered that the Israelite hosts were not invulnerable. This was Joshua's fear, that the Canaanites and all the inhabitants of the land would hear of it, and compass them around, and cut off their name from the earth.

As soon as we have committed sin, we look furtively around to see whether we have been watched; and then we take measures to tie up the consequences which would naturally accrue. Failing this, we are deeply humiliated. Saul was much more moved by his desire for Samuel to worship the Lord with him, and thereby honor him in the presence of the elders of Israel, than by his disobedience to the divine will (1 Sam. 15:30). We dread the consequences of sin more than the sin itself; discovery more than misdoing; what others may say and do more than the look of pain and sorrow on the face that looks out on us from the encircling throng of glorified spirits.

But with God it is not so. It is our sin—one of the most grievous features of which is our failure to recognize its intrinsic evil—that presses him down, as a cart groans beneath its load. The boy grieves because sickness shuts him away from his companions—the excursion on the river; the game in the woods; the swift gliding over the deep blue ice on the ringing skate; but the mother grieves over the disease, of which the burning fever or the labored breath is the symptom. In the heart of the mother, sorrow for the disappointment of the child is almost obliterated by the eager anxiety with which she bends over his bed.

Very few of us realize what sin is, because we have had no experience of a character without it, either in ourselves or in others. People speak of being entirely delivered from sin, but they know not what they say, or whereof they affirm. None that has been born of woman, save One, has ever had the experience of a perfectly sinless character. Babes seem pure as the unfolding lily, which has not been freckled or soiled by contact with earth stains, but they had been purer if . . . ; Christian maidens are sweet and lovely, but they had been lovelier if . . . ; saints seem blameless and harmless, but they had been saintlier if—if they had not been originally connected with a fallen race.

It is, of course, possible to learn something of the exceeding sinfulness of sin by viewing the agony, heartbreak, and shame of the dying Lord; by remembering its infinite cost to the love of God; by recalling the comparisons of Scripture, in which the most loathsome forms of disease are its chosen types; or by considering the worm that never dies, the fire that is never quenched. And yet the true way to a proper realization of sin is to cultivate the friendship of the Holy God. The more we know him, the more utterly we shall enter into his thought about the subtle evil of our heart. We shall find sin lurking where we least anticipated—in our motives; in our religious acts; in our hasty judgment of others; in our lack of tender, sensitive, pitying love; in our censorious condemnation of those who may be restrained by the action of a more sensitive conscience than our own, from claiming all that we claim to possess. We shall learn that every look, tone, gesture, word, thought which is not consistent with perfect love indicates that the virus of sin has not yet been expelled from our nature; and we shall come to mourn not so much for the results of sin as for the sin itself. This is the godly sorrow that needs not to be repented of. Here are tears which angels catch in God's tear-bottles. In hours like these we approach most nearly the world where sin is hated—not because it cost us Paradise, for that has been more than replaced, but because it is *sin.*

2. WE SHOULD SUBMIT OURSELVES TO THE JUDGMENT OF GOD. "And the Lord said unto Joshua, Get thee up; wherefore liest thou thus upon thy face?" It was as if he had said, "Thou grievest for the effect; grieve rather for the cause. I am well able to preserve my people from the assaults of their foes, though all Canaan beset them; and I am equally able to maintain the honor of my name. These are not the main matters for concern: but that a worm is already gnawing at the root of the gourd, and a plague is already eating out the vitals of the people whom I have redeemed. With my right arm I will screen you from attack, while you give yourselves to the investigation and destruction of the accursed thing."

Whenever there is perpetual failure in our life, we may be sure that there is some secret evil lurking in heart and life. It may not always be possible for us to go direct to the spot where the evil has made its lair. But we may be sure that there is an accursed thing somewhere in our midst, and that therefore we cannot stand before our enemies. Somewhere there is a fault in the insulation of the wire through which the currents of divine power and grace come to us; and it is useless to pray that they may be renewed until we have repaired the defect. Much of the time spent in public and private prayer would be better employed by subjecting our dealings with each other and our walk before God to a searching scrutiny. It is a mistake to be on the face pleading with God for a blessing—and especially for the blessing of Pentecost—while there is some evil thing in our hearts needing to be dealt with before the divine energies can come to us. It is not a question of God's willingness or unwillingness, but of the laws of the spiritual world, which make him unable to ally himself with consciously permitted sin.

Have you, reader, been beaten back in your Christian work, or exposed to perpetual defeat by some petty temptation? Then it would be well to call a halt—not to hold a prayer meeting, but to order your heart-life before God. Thus, if you cannot discern the evil thing that lies at the root of your trouble, he may discern it for you—he whose eyes are as a flame of fire, and in whose hand is a sharp sword.

(a) In searching out the causes of failure, we must be *willing to know the worst*; and this is almost the hardest condition. Ostrich-like, we all hide our heads in the sand from unwelcome tidings. It is the voice of an iron resolution, or of mature Christian experience, that can say without faltering, "Let me know the worst." But as we bare ourselves to the good Physician, let us remember that he is our husband; that his eyes film with love and pity; that he desires to indicate the source of our sorrow only to remove it—so that for him and for us there may be the vigor of perfect soul health and consequent bliss.

He will communicate the result of his search by methods which are known to his delicate tenderness. Do not get into a fever. Do not rush from one to another for advice. Do not bewilder yourself with trying to detect his voice amid the tumult of voices that are sure to clamor for hearing when you bend down your ear to listen. "Be still and know." The responsibility of showing you your mistake is wholly with him, if you have placed all in his hands. Leave it there and wait. If he has anything to say, he will say it clearly, unmistakably, and certainly. If he says nothing, it is because the set time has not come. But tomorrow, in the morning, it may be, he will speak to you and tell you all. In the meanwhile, wait and trust.

(b) When God deals with sin, he *traces back its geneology.* Notice the particularity with which, twice over, the sacred historian gives the list of Achan's progenitors. It is always, "Achan, the son of Carmi, the son of Zabdi, the son of Zerah, of the tribe of Judah" (7:1,16–18).

There, in the early morning, Joshua and Phinehas stood to discern the transgressor with the aid of the Urim and Thummim of Judgment. The princes of Israel passed before them first; and the prince of Judah was taken. Then the clans of Judah; and that of the Zarhites was taken. Then the Zarhites; and the family of Zabdi was taken. And then Achan. How his heart must have stood still, as he saw the inevitable closing in of his destiny—like the contracting walls of a chamber of horrors on a hapless victim!

But sin is sporadic. To deal with it thoroughly, we need to go back to its parentage. All who have carefully watched the processes of the inner life bear witness, that a long period will often intervene between the first germ of sin, in a permitted thought or glance of evil, and its flower or fruit in act. We generally deal with the wrong that flames out before the sight of our fellows; we should go behind to the spark as it lay smoldering for hours before, and to the carelessness which left it there. We only awake when the rock disintegrates and threatens to fall upon our cottage roof; God would lead us back to the moment when a tiny seed, borne on the breeze, floating through the air, found a lodgment in some crevice of our heart, and which, although the soil was scanty, succeeded in keeping its foothold till it had struck down its tiny roots, and gathered strength enough to split the rock which had given it welcome. And by this insight into small beginnings, our God would forearm us against great catastrophes.

What we call sin is the outcome of sin permitted days, perhaps weeks before—which, in the meanwhile, had been gathering strength within the heart. An avalanche is the result of the dislocation of a few flakes of snow which had fluttered from their place weeks earlier before overwhelming the villagers and smothering them in their beds. There is reason therefore for the advice of the wise man: "Keep *thy heart* above all that thou guardest;

for out of it are the issues of life" (R.V. margin). If we would be kept clear from great transgression, we must see to it that we are cleared from hidden faults, so subtle and microscopic that they would elude any but a conscience kept sensitive by the grace of the Holy Spirit.

In the light of these thoughts we shall better understand what is meant by one of the deepest passages in the Epistles. James tells us—and none could better discourse on such a theme than the saintly president of the apostolic Church—that "Each man is tempted when he is drawn away by his own lust, and enticed." A word which surely suggests that temptation is not wholly a matter outside the soul, as some think! And he goes on to say, "The lust, when it hath conceived, beareth sin; and the sin, when it is full grown, bringeth forth death." Mark those words, *when it hath conceived, beareth;* they are very deep. In nature there is an interval, a period of incubation.

If, therefore, you have fled before Ai, do not be content when you have discovered Achan; but continue your search till you have learned what gave him power to hurt you, and so work your way through the links in the long chain till you discover his remote ancestor in something which you did not suspect for the moment, but which was the guilty progenitor. Achan's own words shall enforce the necessity: "I saw . . . I coveted . . . I took."

(c) It is a good thing at times to *muster the clans of heart and life.* We must make the principal tribes of our being pass before God—the public, and private; our behavior in the business, the family, the church—until one of them is taken. Then examine that department, going through its various aspects and engagements, analyzing it in days, or duties; resolving it into its various elements; and scrutinizing each. The auditor of accounts in some great business house, called in to discover the source of leakage, will for obvious reasons eliminate from his inquiry certain of the ledgers representing the more prosperous branches of the trade; and thus he narrows his inquiries within a smaller and yet smaller range.

This duty of self-examination should be pursued by those who have least relish for it, as most likely they really need it; while those who are naturally of an introspective disposition will probably apply themselves to the task without being reminded of the necessity of so doing, and should guard against its excess and abuse. Whoever undertakes it should do so in reliance on the Holy Spirit; and give ten glances to the blessed Lord for every one that is taken at the corruptions of the natural heart. It is "looking off unto Jesus" which is the real secret of soul growth.

3. WE SHOULD HOLD NO PARLEY WITH DISCOVERED SIN. "And Joshua, and all Israel with him, took Achan, the son of Zerah, and the silver, and the mantle, and the wedge of gold, and his sons, and his daughters, and his oxen, and his asses, and his sheep, and his tent, and all that he had. And they brought them up unto the Valley of Achor. And all Israel stoned him with stones; and they burned them with fire, after they had stoned them with stones." Then Jehovah repeated to Joshua the words which had preceded the capture of Jericho, "Fear not . . . see, I have given into thy hand the king of Ai, and his people, and his city, and his land."

So by the Lord's command Joshua sent by night a large contingent of men to lie in ambush between Bethel and Ai. Then up the long defile Joshua marched with more mighty men of valor. There was a sense in every breast of an integrity which had put away all cause of failure and defeat. The preparations were skillfully made; the appearance of flight on the part of Israel drew forth the men of Ai to headlong pursuit; and the city was left at the mercy of the ambush, which at the sign of Joshua's uplifted javelin arose, entered the city, and set it on fire. And in that very place where Israel had met with so disastrous a defeat, the people took great spoil, especially of cattle, which they drove down in triumph to the camp at Gilgal.

God never reveals an evil which he does not require us to remove. And if heart and flesh fail, if our hand refuses to obey our faltering will, if the paralysis of evil has so far enfeebled us that we cannot lift the stone, or wield the knife, or strike the flint-stones for the fire, then he will do for us what must be done, but which we cannot do. Some are cast in a mold so strong that they can dare to raise the hatchet, and cut off the arm just madly bitten, and before poison has passed from it into the system; others must await the surgeon's knife. But the one lesson for all regarding the inner life is to be willing for God to do his work in us, through us, or for us.

So the Valley of Achor (meaning "trouble") becomes "the Door of Hope" (Hosea 2:15). From that sterile, mountain-guarded valley, Israel marched to victory; or, to use the highly colored imagery of Hosea, it was as though the massive slabs opened in the cliffs, and the people passed into fields, vineyards, and oliveyards, singing amid their rich luxuriance as they sang in their youth, in the day when they came up out of Egypt. Ah, metaphor as true as fair! For all our inner life, there is no Valley of Achor where the work of execution is faithfully performed in which there is not a door of hope— entrance into the garden of the Lord—and a song so sweet, so joyous, so triumphant, that it would seem as if the buoyancy of youth were wed with the experience and mellowness of age.

11

EBAL AND GERIZIM

(JOSHUA 8:30–35)

"Therefore, child of mortality,
    love thou the merciful Father!
Wish what the Holy One wishes!—
    and not from fear but affection:
Fear is the virtue of slaves;
    but the heart that loveth is willing;
Perfect was before God,—and perfect is—
    Love and Love only!"

LONGFELLOW

T HIS was one of the most impressive scenes that occurred during the occupation of Canaan. Jericho and Ai were heaps of blackened ruins, their kings and people utterly destroyed, their dependent villages mute with terror. All through the land the rumor ran of the might of Israel's God. And beyond the horizon of the visible, into those realms of evil spirits which had too long filled the chosen land with horrid rite and obscene orgy, surely tidings came that struck the knell of their supremacy. There must have been panic there, in those dark realms, like that which Milton, in his sublime "Ode to the Nativity," ascribes to the hour of the birth of Christ.

The nations of Canaan appear to have been so panic-stricken that they offered no resistance, and made no attempt at molestation, as all Israel went on a pilgrimage of thirty miles to perform a religious duty—which had been distinctly, and more than once, commanded by the great Lawgiver whose words constituted their supreme directory.

"It shall be," so the word stood, "on the day when ye shall pass over Jordan unto the land which the Lord thy God giveth thee, that thou shalt set thee up great stones, and plaster them with plaster, and thou shalt write upon them all the words of this law" (Deut. 11:26–32; 27:2–3). Joshua lost no time in obeying these minute and urgent injunctions; and within two or three days after the fall of Ai—perhaps within three weeks of the crossing of the Jordan—the people were assembled in the valley of Shechem. This valley lies from east to west, sentineled on the north by the sterile slopes of Ebal, rearing itself gaunt and barren against the intense blue of the Eastern sky, and on the south by its twin giant Gerizim, "a majestic mass of limestone, with stately head and precipitous sides, but fruitful and picturesque, girt with foliage and beauty."

The valley between these two is one of the most beautiful in Palestine. Jacob's well lies at its mouth; and all its luxuriant extent is covered with the verdant beauty of gardens, and orchards, and olive groves, rolling in waves of billowy beauty up to the walls of Shechem; while the murmur of brooks flowing in all directions fills the air. The width of the valley is about a third of a mile; though the summits of the two mountains, in the lap of which it lies, are two miles apart. It is remarkable that where the two mountains face each other and touch most closely, with a green valley of five hundred yards between, each is hollowed out, and the limestone stratum is broken into a succession of ledges, "so as to present the appearance of a series of regular benches." Thus a natural amphitheater is formed, capable of containing a vast audience of people; and the acoustic properties are so perfect in that dry and rainless air that Canon Tristram speaks of two of his party taking up positions on the opposite mountains, reciting the Ten Commandments antiphonally, and hearing each other perfectly.

To this place Joshua led the people, that, by a solemn act, they might take possession of the land for God.

1. THE ALTAR ON EBAL. Ebal was stern and barren in its aspect. There was a congruity, therefore, between its appearance and the part it played in the solemn proceedings of the day. For far up its slopes gathered the dense masses of the six tribes, who, with thunderous Amens twelve times repeated, answered the voices of the band of white-robed Levites, as, standing with Joshua and the elders and officers and judges in the green valley, they solemnly repeated the curses of the law.

But that was not the first proceeding in the holy ceremonial. Before the people took up their assigned places on the mountain sides, an altar was reared on the lower slopes of Ebal. Special directions as to its construction had been given in Deuteronomy 27. It was to be built of unhewn stones, on which no iron tool had been lifted; probably to guard against any attempt to set forth the likeness of God, and to discountenance the florid and lascivious ornamentations of which the surrounding heathen were so fond.

There they offered burnt offerings, and sacrificed peace offerings. The *burnt offering* was what was known as a sweet savor offering. The whole of the victim was burned. It was "an offering made by fire, of a sweet savor unto the Lord" (Lev. 1:9). Herein the Holy Spirit signified, secondarily, our duty to present ourselves without reserve to God; but primarily the devotion of our blessed Lord to accomplish his Father's will in our redemption. He held nothing back; there was no reserve. He emptied himself, and he did it ungrudgingly; for he said, "I delight to do thy will, O my God." How sweet this was to the heart of the Father! If on the one hand there was anguish such as only God could feel, on the other there was the gratification of delighted love.

The *peace offering* also belonged to the sweet savor offerings, but it was not wholly consumed; a part was eaten by the offerers, to testify that in it they had fellowship and communion with God. In the sight, therefore, of Israel, Joshua and other chosen representatives partook of portions of the sacrifices, and obeyed the divine injunction, "Thou shalt eat there, and thou shalt rejoice before the Lord thy God." If any of the native Hittites, peering out from behind great boulders, were spectators of that scene, they must have been impressed with the thought that Jehovah delighted in the happiness of his people, and that his service was as the scent of clover, or as the feast of children at their father's table. We feed on the peace offering when we meditate on the love and death of our blessed Lord, and enter into some of the Father's thoughts of satisfaction at the work he did, and the spirit in which he did it.

As we pass into the Land of Promise we must see to it that we do not leave behind the devout and loving consideration of that precious blood by which we have been redeemed and which is our life. Our highest and most rapturous experiences can never take the place of this. Constantly we must remind ourselves and others that we are redeemed sinners; and that all our hopes of salvation, our fellowship with God, our motives for service, are derived from what our Saviour did when he bore our sins in his own body on the tree.

Since he died there, we need never stand on the mount of cursing. Because he counted not his life dear to himself, those gaunt and forbidding slopes have become the scene of blessed communion with God. We sit and feast with him, and from peak to peak joy chases the terrors of the curse; and smiles look out on us from the old rocks, while the torrents tinged with the light of the sun flash and sing. Because he shed his blood, there shall, unlike the field of Gilboa, be "dew, and rain, and fields of offerings," even on Ebal; until its terraced slopes resemble those of the opposite mount of blessing. Ah, blessed Lord, how shall we thank you, who has redeemed us from the curse of the law, and made Ebal so choice a trysting-place with God!

2. THE LAW IN CANAAN. Around the altar strong men reared great stones, and plastered them with a facing of cement, composed of lime or gypsum, on which it was easy to write all the words of the law very plainly (Deut. 27:8). In that dry air, where there is no frost to split and disintegrate, such inscriptions—graven on the soft cement, or written on its polished surface when dry with ink or paint, as in the case of the monumental stones of Egypt—would remain for centuries. As the time could not have sufficed for the inscription of the whole law, it is probable that the more salient points were alone committed to the custody of those great cromlechs, to perpetuate to later generations the conditions of the tenure on which Israel held the lease of Palestine. They were a standing protest against the sins which had blighted those fertile valleys, and an incentive to the obedience on which so much of the future hinged.

But when we turn from the literal to the metaphorical, and ask for the underlying typical meaning of this inscription of the law in so prominent a position in the Land of Promise, we are at first startled. What can it mean? Is there a connection after all between law and grace? Are those who sit with Christ in heavenly places still amenable to law—"under the law," as the apostle puts it? Is it not true that, by our union with Christ who died, we have passed out of the sphere in which we were married to our first husband, the law, and have left it behind us? Are we not, therefore, discharged from the law of our former husband and married to another, even to him that was raised from the dead?

There is but one answer to all these questions. We have

died to the covenant wherein we were holden. We serve in newness of the spirit, and not in oldness of the letter. We are not looking to our obedience to merit the favor of God, or to win any of the blessings of the gospel. But it is also true that faith does not make the law of God of none effect; and still, in the Land of Promise, he undertakes to write it clearly on the tablets of our hearts. In each one of us there is an Ebal with its altar and its stones. The soul comes back again and again to those first principles of the perfect life; not by compulsion from without, but by the impulse of the Holy Spirit.

The case is this. When we yield ourselves entirely to the Spirit of life which is in Christ Jesus, and which passes freely through us, as the blood through artery and vein, he makes us very sensitive to the least commandment or desire of him whom he has taught us to love; we dread to see the shadow of suffering pass over his face more than to feel the pang of remorse rend our hearts; we find our heaven in his smile of approval, and the "Well done!" that glistens in his eyes when we have done anything for the least of his children; we are conscious of the pulse of a love which he has instilled, and which supplies us with the highest code for life. And so, insensibly, while we yield ourselves to him we find ourselves keeping the law after a fashion which was foreign to us when it was a mere outward observance; and we cry with the Psalmist, "Oh, how love I thy law! it is my meditation all the day."

3. THE CONVOCATION. When these rites were fulfilled, the third and concluding scene of this extraordinary transaction took place. In the center of the valley the ark rested, with its group of attendant priests and Levites. Hard by, Joshua and the leaders of the tribes, elders, officers, and judges. Then up the slopes of Ebal, finding seats on its terraced sides, were Reuben, Gad and Asher, and Zebulun, Dan and Naphtali; while up the slopes of Gerizim were the larger and more important tribes of Simeon, and Levi, and Judah, and Issachar,

and Joseph, and Benjamin. It was as though the voice of blessing must be louder than that of cursing—a prediction of its final prevalence and triumph.

Then Joshua read aloud "all the words of the law, the blessings and cursings, according to all that is written in the book of the law. There was not a word of all that Moses commanded, which Joshua read not before all the assembly of Israel, and the women, and the little ones, and the strangers that were conversant among them." And as he solemnly read, whether the blessing or the curse, each respective item was responded to by the Amens that thundered forth from thousands of throats, and rolled in reverberating echoes through the hills. Earth has seldom heard such shouts as those!

It is well worth our while to ponder the list of blessings appended to obedience in that memorable twenty-eighth chapter of Deuteronomy, that we may discover their spiritual counterparts, and, having found them, to claim them.

Let us, first, be quite sure that we are right with God; next, that we are on his plan and doing his will; also thirdly, that we are set upon his glory, altogether irrespective of our own interests; and we shall find ourselves able to appropriate blessings of which we little dreamed. The Lord will open his good treasury in heaven and make us plenteous for good, and establish us for a holy people unto himself.

Nor can we better close our meditation than by asking that the Holy Spirit may so indwell and guide us that we may choose what he ordains, and not swerve by a hair's breadth to the right or left of the narrow path of obedience; keeping his commandments; obeying his biddings; perfectly conformed to his will. Thus shall Ebal cease to frown, and Gerizim rain its blessings upon us. Ours shall be the Beatitudes with which our Master opened his great discourse. Ours, the heavenly Kingdom, the divine comfort, the earthly inheritance, the filling and the mercy, the vision of God, and the blessed prerogative of sonship, and finally the great reward (Matt. 5:1–12).

12

THE WILES OF THE DEVIL

(JOSHUA 9)

"The perils that we well might shun
  We saunter forth to meet;
The path into the road of sin
  We tread with careless feet.
The air that comes instinct with death—
  We bid it round us flow;
And when our hands should bar the gate
  We parley with the foe!"

BRIGHT

THE whole country was in arms. Minor differences were obliterated, a truce was given to tribal wars, and those who had been deadly foes were driven by the very necessities of the case into a combination against the dreaded invader. Just as the Pharisees and Sadducees, who were hereditary foes, combined to destroy Christ, so did all the kings—whether Hittite or Amorite, Perizzite or Hivite—gather themselves together to fight with Israel and with Joshua, "with one accord." In front of that common danger all minor contentions held their peace.

Tidings of this formidable coalition found their way into the camp of Gilgal, whither leader and people had recently returned from their pilgrimage to Shechem.

Probably Joshua heard the tidings without great dismay; but to the princes it was welcome news to learn almost simultaneously that there was the possibility of forming a league with a people who were likely to stand by them at that solemn juncture. This league, however, was to cost them as much anxiety, if not more, as the sin of Achan.

Whenever we are threatened with unprecedented difficulty, we may expect to encounter just such a temptation as that which the Gibeonites presented to Israel.

1. "THEY DID WORK WILILY." One day a strange spectacle presented itself at the gates of the camp. A group of strangers announced themselves, who seemed to have come from a far country. In every article of dress, as well as in the trappings of their asses, there were the signs of long journeys. Their shoes were mended; their garments faded; their sacks in holes; their wine-skins patched; and when they brought out the remnants of their bread, the mold suggested the days that had passed since it left the oven. All the camp gathered to see them enter; and as they passed through the lines of eager spectators, from one to another the word passed, "Who are they? Whence came they? Wherever they come from, they are evidently foreigners to this country." Compassion would be freely expended on them for the weary fatigue of their travel; and no one suspected for a moment that beneath the clever disguise was concealed a band of Hivites. But so it was. For the first time, within the precincts of the camp which was holy unto the Lord, there stood a company of those inhabitants of Canaan which Israel had been expressly commissioned to destroy.

Had it not been for their disguise they would not have been permitted to come within the circle of the tents. A cry of horror would have passed from lip to lip, drowning any attempt of theirs to speak; but their story was so reasonable, their references to Jehovah so reverential, their appearance so in keeping with the account they gave of themselves, that they threw Joshua, princes, and people completely off their guard.

It is in this way that we are tempted still—more by the wiles of Satan than by his open assaults; more by the deceitfulness of sin than by its declared war. And it is little matter for wonder that those who succeed at Jericho and Ai fall into the nets woven and laid down by the wiles of Gibeon. Better to meet Caiaphas than Judas. A black devil is less to be dreaded than a white one.

Take up the chronicles of the early Church. With no prestige, or wealth, or human learning to help her, she swept forward on her beneficent mission, during the first centuries of her existence, freeing the slave, lifting woman from her degradation, smiting down gigantic systems of idolatry and philosophy, and winning myriads of trophies for Jesus Christ. There was no reason to doubt that she would speedily accomplish the will of her divine Founder in encompassing the world with the tidings of redemption, and proclaiming his gospel to every creature. All through these days each step was taken at a great cost of agony and blood. The kings of the earth set themselves in array, and the rulers were gathered together against the Lord, and against his Christ. Ten awful persecutions rolled up against the Ark, threatening to engulf it in their blood-red waters. The great dragon persecuted the woman; and the serpent cast out of his mouth after her water as a river, that he might cause her to be carried away by the stream.

But the effect of all this was most salutary. There was no temptation to hypocrites to join the ranks of the faithful; and these counted not their lives dear unto themselves, if only by word and life they might commend the gospel of their Lord. Those were the days when the saints walked the earth in white, and God was not ashamed to be called their God, and men were attracted by the sheen of a celestial beauty.

Then, since the adversary could not prevail by force, he

resorted to deceit. Constantine was his agent, through whom an alliance was effected between the new, young faith and the expiring systems of paganism. The great fasts of the Christian faith were commemorated on the days consecrated from time immemorial to heathen festivals, and after a while in the garments and with the rites by which those festivals had been signalized. A league was formed between the Church and the world; between truth and falsehood; between the new and the old. The religion of Jesus Christ struck hands in solemn covenant with the old and mended shoes, the old garments, and the moldy provision of Babylonish idolatry.

From that moment a change passed over the Church of Christ. What she gained in prestige of worldly power she lost in character and spiritual strength. From that moment the course of the professing Church has been always downward; and today it is her weakness and shame that she has so unaccountable a liking for the old relics of a defunct paganism.

Many a soul that has withstood the attacks of the more pronounced forms of temptation has succumbed before the treacherous arts of the flatterer. Young Christians have much to fear from those who introduce themselves as being also religious, and as enthusiastic as they, and who proceed to urge them "not to overdo it." We all have to beware of those insinuating themselves into our affections, our counsels, our homes, or our businesses who assume an interest in religion which they do not feel; who talk glibly and falsely of the fame of God; and who offer to do all in their power to further and help our interests while they are plotting our ruin. There are plenty of Gibeonites about. "Beloved, believe not every spirit; but prove the spirits, whether they are of God; because many false prophets are gone out into the world" (R.V.). "Bear with me. . . . I fear, lest by any means, as the serpent beguiled Eve in his craftiness, your minds should be corrupted from the simplicity and the purity that is toward Christ" (R.V.).

2. "THEY ASKED NOT COUNSEL OF THE LORD." The leaders of Israel seem at first to have been a little suspicious of their visitors. "And the men of Israel said unto the Hivites, Peradventure ye dwell among us, and how shall we make a covenant with you?" But their suspicions were allayed as they listened to their story, and saw the apparent evidences of their long journey. Here surely was an opportunity of proving their sagacity. They had not been allowed as yet to show their bravery and might, but they could at least now give proof of their superior insight! This was altogether too obvious a matter to need to be referred to Phinehas with his Urim and Thummim! And so they sampled their provisions, moldy as they were, in token of their willingness to count them allies and friends; indeed, the princes of the congregation sware unto them. But they "asked not counsel at the mouth of the Lord."

What an ominous sound there is in those words! They portend disaster—and it befell. Up to this moment the initiative had always been taken by the Lord. Now for the first time it is taken by Joshua and the people. In all the previous chapters the words run thus: "And the Lord said unto Joshua"; but there is no such phrase in this. Israel through her chosen leaders acted for herself, and easily fell into the trap. If only they had inquired of the Lord, the dimming light in the sacred stone would have betrayed the fatal secret and arrested the formation of the league.

Let us lay the moral to our heart. Earth's somber tints and cross-lights are very perplexing; and it is often extremely hard to detect the truth. The foolish virgins are so much like the wise; the tares so resemble the wheat; the hireling imitates so precisely the Shepherd's voice; the devil's mimicry of an angel of light is so exact; By-path Meadow is parted from the King's Highway by so narrow a boundary. We urgently need, as the apostle prayed for his Philippian converts, that we may have not only all knowledge, but all discernment, so that we may "prove the things that differ" (Phil. 1:10, R.V. margin).

In one place this power to discriminate is said to result from use (Heb. 5:14), while in the passage already quoted it is attributed to an abounding love. But following the suggestion of the narrative before us, we may say that it will follow naturally on the careful cultivation of the habit of asking counsel at the mouth of the Lord.

Never trust your own judgment. When your common sense is most sure of the rightness of a certain course of action, it will be best to make assurance doubly sure by lifting up your soul to God, that it may dim with his No, or glisten with his Yes. When voices within or without would hasten you to decide on the strength of your own conclusions, then be careful to refer the whole matter from the lower court of your own judgment to the supreme tribunal of God's. If there is any doubt or hesitation left after such reference, be sure that as yet the time has not come for you to understand all God's will. Under such circumstances—wait. Throw the responsibility of the pause, and all it may involve, on God; and dare still to wait. As a traveler over the hills, when the mist has come down, elects to stand or lie where it overtakes him, rather than wander on, perhaps to the brink of a precipice—so wait. If you trust God absolutely, it is for him to give you clear directions as to what you should do. And when the time for action arrives, he will have given you such unmistakable indications of his will that you will not be able to mistake them or err therein. "None of them that wait on him shall be ashamed."

Life is full of difficulties. The pointed spear awaits the unwary at the bottom of the pit, the top of which is covered by a slight film of earth. The snare of the fowler, the pestilence that walketh in darkness, the net privily laid, the decoy-bird, the devil in the wily serpent form— of these we need to beware. But prayer is like the spear of Ithuriel*; and before its touch evil will be compelled to show itself in its native deformity, so that we may be thrown instantly upon the watch.

Before entering into any alliance—taking a partner in life, going into a business with another, yielding assent to any proposition which involves confederation with others—be sure to ask counsel at the mouth of the Lord. He will assuredly answer by an irresistible impulse—by the voice of a friend; by a circumstance strange and unexpected; by a passage of Scripture. He will choose his own messenger; but he will send a message.

3. "HEWERS OF WOOD AND DRAWERS OF WATER." There are some oaths better in the breach than the observance, as would have been the case with Herod's.† And if there had been certain peril that these Hivites would corrupt Israel, it had been better for them, notwithstanding the oath of the princes, to have been cut off like the rest of the Canaanites. But all danger of this peril accruing was carefully guarded against by their reduction to servitude. "Hewers of wood and drawers of water, for the congregation and for the altar of Jehovah." This position they retained; and in later years heavy disasters befell Israel because Saul, in his mad zeal, broke the solemn league and covenant into which Joshua and the princes had entered with them (2 Sam. 21:1-2).

This is a beautiful and comforting example of the way in which God overrules our mistakes, and brings blessing out of our sins; as the chemist obtains his loveliest dyes from the refuse of gas retorts. Inadvertently, and without due consideration, some reader may have entered into alliance with a Gibeonite—whether in marriage, in business, or in some other sphere. Are they therefore to abandon their high privilege, and forsake their lofty ministry to the world? Must they cease to be God's portion, and the priests of

---

* In *Paradise Lost.*   † Matthew 14:6–10.

men? Not necessarily. Let them turn to God in repentance and confession, and he will teach them how these very hindrances may become great means of help; so that they shall hew the wood for the burnt offering, draw the water for the libations, and promote the prosperity and well-being of the soul. "Out of the eater shall come forth meat, and out of the strong shall come forth sweetness."

"If any brother hath an unbelieving wife, and she is content to dwell with him, let him not leave her. And the woman which hath an unbelieving husband, and he is content to dwell with her, let her not leave her husband. For the unbelieving husband is sanctified in the wife, and the unbelieving wife is sanctified in the brother. . . . How knowest thou, O wife, whether thou shalt save thy husband? Or how knowest thou, O husband, whether thou shalt save thy wife? But God hath called us in peace" (1 Cor. 7:12–16, R.V.).

It is very sweet to think of the grace of God which forgives our sins as being the preliminary condition to transforming the results of those sins to blessing. How often, in the lives of God's saints, the ancient prediction has been realized, that instead of the thorn should come up the fir tree, and instead of the briar the myrtle tree, that these may be to the Lord for a name and an everlasting sign.

It is true that the natural consequences of our sin may have to run their course. The hand of the reclaimed drunkard will still tremble. The constitution of the prodigal will never be able to throw off the effects of the fever contracted from the swine-troughs. The Gibeonite will always, in this world at least, be tied to you. But these things shall not rule, but serve; shall not impede, but promote. They shall hew the wood and draw the water for the inner shrine of character, and for the promotion of the loftiest standard of Christian attainment.

13

A MEMORABLE DAY

(JOSHUA 10:14)

> "This day shall shine,
> For evermore
> To thee a star divine
> On Time's dark shore."
> A. PROCTOR

"THERE was no day like that." It stood alone in the history of the conquest, and of Joshua. Let us notice these points:

1. THE CONFEDERACY WHICH WAS GATHERED AGAINST ISRAEL. Israel had previously dealt with separate cities, Jericho and Ai; but now five kings of the Amorites joined together, namely, the kings of Jerusalem, Hebron, Jarmuth, Lachish, and Eglon.

The traitor city of Gibeon was the object of the attack of the combined forces; partly because its defection had aroused the fiercest animosity of its former allies, and partly that by its occupation they might be able to interpose one further barrier to the invasion of the Israelites. This was more especially the purpose of Adonizedek, whose name, "lord of righteousness," recalls the ancient glory of Melchizedek, the friend of Abram. The royal city of Gibeon lay only six miles to the north of

121

Jerusalem.

Suddenly, the men of Gibeon found themselves surrounded by a vast host of infuriated warriors, who, not daring to measure themselves against Joshua, because of the awe which his exploits had inspired, were all the more eager to wreak their vengeance upon those who had dared to make a league with him. Relying upon Joshua's fidelity to the covenant so recently formed, a message was sent in breathless haste, summoning him to their help.

2. JOSHUA'S HEROIC FAITH. There had been great days in his life before: the day of the Passover, when he had crossed the Red Sea at the forefront of his tribe; the day of the fight with Amalek when, beneath the uplifted hands of Moses, he drove the tribes of the desert before him; the day when first he had stood with his master amid the burning splendor of the vision of God; the day when he had returned with Caleb from espying the land, and had heard himself singled out to survive his nation and to enter the Land of Promise. There had also been some wonderful days lately, when he crossed the Jordan, saw the Angel, and beheld the walls of Jericho fall flat; but there had never been a day in his life quite like this.

It was a day of vigor. As soon as he received the message, he saw the importance of at once vindicating the trust reposed in him. Before the sun went down, orders had passed through the camp that the men of war should be ready for a midnight march; and at dead of night he climbed the pass from Gilgal to Gibeon—fifteen difficult miles—and came upon the sleeping host suddenly before they had had time to prepare themselves for fight. Inertness and indolence ill become those who are entrusted with great concerns. The stirring of God's Spirit in man makes the pulse throb quickly; purposes form themselves in the will, and all the nature is braced, and knit, to subserve the heroic soul.

It was a day of fellowship. Soon after the first message had come, with surely a certain amount of startling surprise, God had spoken to him and said, "Fear them not, for I have delivered them into thy hands; there shall not a man of them stand before thee." It was in the strength of that promise, and under the pressure of such stirring circumstances, that he soon spoke to God as man had never spoken before.

There must have been hard fighting all the morning. It was dawn when the battle began, and it would have been toward afternoon when the kings gave the signal for retreat; and the Canaanites, unable longer to sustain the successive onsets of Israel, charging to the battle cry of "Jehovah, mighty in battle," broke into flight like a flock of panic-stricken sheep. Ten miles they fled, climbing a precipitous ascent to the high ridge of Beth-horon the Upper. From that point the road drops, broken and rugged, seven hundred feet in two miles. The rock is cut into steps. Down this breakneck steep the fugitives fled, to reach, if only they might, their fastnesses and citadels, which lay in the valley below, and longing for night to put a pause upon the anguish of the pursuit. It was at this point that the storm, of which we will speak presently, burst on them with irresistible fury, as if the whole artillery of heaven had suddenly opened fire, and when Joshua reached the head of the ravine, before him the descent was blocked with the masses of the routed armies; beneath him the valley was thick with cloud, which was venting its contents on his foes; while upward to him there surged the mingled voice of the cry of the vanquished, the shout of the pursuer, and the chorus of the hailstones. Behind him, over the hills of Gibeon, the sun was westering. It wanted but an hour or two, and its sudden disappearance would bring on the rapid Eastern twilight, while the moon's pale face appearing over the purple waters of the Great Sea was waiting to lead on the night.

It was under these circumstances that Joshua dared to ask an unprecedented gift of God—that the day might be prolonged. "Why should not the sun, which is thy creature, but worshiped too long in this land in thy stead, now subserve thy purpose in the destruction of these who have given it what was thy due? And why should not yonder moon, which has so often looked down upon these licentious orgies of the Amorites, now see their impurity washed out by blood? They are thine, Jehovah; they will perform thy bidding; hearken to my voice and let them stay."

There are high days in human lives when thought and purpose, which had been quietly gathering strength, suddenly leap from their leash, like waters swelling against a barrier, and vent themselves in acts or words or prayers. We are not, then, drunk with wine: but we are flushed, as to our spirits, with the exhilaration and sense of power which the Spirit of God alone can give; or, to put it in another form, we catch fire. There is too little of this capacity of rising into the loftiest experience of that spirit life which is within the reach of us all, through living fellowship with God: but whenever we realize and use it, it is as when the feeble, smoldering wick is plunged into oxygen gas; or as when a flower that had struggled against the frost is placed in the tropical atmosphere of the hothouse. In such hours we realize what Jesus meant when he said, "Whosoever shall say unto this mountain, be thou taken up and cast into the sea; and shall not doubt in his heart, but shall believe that what he saith cometh to pass; he shall have it."

It was a day of triumphant onlook. Discomfited, weary, vanquished, the kings sheltered in the cave of Makkedah; but Joshua did not stay to dispatch them; he was too eager to finish what he had commenced, and to prevent the Canaanites from reentering their cities. So he took measures for keeping them imprisoned in the cave till his return. Presently, flushed with victory, and with (as Josephus tells us) the loss of hardly a single life, he came again. The kings were summoned from their hiding place; and as they crouched abjectly at the feet of their conquerors, Joshua called for all the men of Israel, and said unto the chiefs of the men of war, "Come near, put your feet upon the necks of these kings." And while they stood in that attitude of unquestioned victory, there broke on the exalted spirit-kindled imagination of the warrior-chieftain the sure prevision of the ultimate issue of the conflict in which they were engaged. He already saw the day when every knee would bow before Jehovah's might; when every king would be prostrate before Israel's arm; and when the whole land would be subdued. So all through the years that followed, he would come back again and again in thought to that moment when he stood on a peak of the mountain of vision, and said, "Fear not, nor be dismayed; be strong and of good courage; for thus shall the Lord do to all your enemies against whom ye fight."

3. THE EXTRAORDINARY INTERPOSITION OF JEHOVAH. The storm that broke in that late afternoon over the rugged descent to Beth-horon was no common one. Middle Eastern hailstones are of great size: it is said that sometimes lumps of ice, of a pound or more in weight, will fall; and these would naturally kill any on whom they fell. But the remarkable thing in this case was that the storm broke in a moment when its fury could be spent on the Amorites without inflicting injury upon Israel. "It came to pass as they fled from before Israel, while they were in the going down of Beth-horon, that the Lord cast down great stones from heaven upon them unto Azekah, and they died; they were more that died with the hailstones than they whom the children of Israel slew with the sword."

But the stupendous miracle of the day consisted in the arrest of daylight. It is obvious that verses 12–15 are a quotation from the poetical book of Jasher.* This is

---

* Note verse 13. See also 2 Samuel 1:18.

clear, because verse 15 is duplicate with verse 43; and the style is altogether different from the majestic roll of the historian's prose. But there is no reason to believe, with some, that these verses give us only a metaphorical account of the fight, and of the thoroughness of the victory; as though the poet would say that in that one day Israel did the work of two. Beneath the veil of poetry, introduced here by the historian, there must be a reference to a marvelous and miraculous episode.

We place no limit to the divine power. He who made all things is the Monarch of all. It is indeed easy for him to impose his will on nature, man, or human will. The miracle of the resurrection is so stupendous in the raising of our human nature, incorporate with the divine, to take its place in the heart of the forces of the spirit-world, that we need not hesitate to accept any well accredited marvel. Nor should we scruple to believe that God could make the clock of the universe stop, if it were necessary that it should do so.

But it is not necessary to believe that he did this. No doubt here, as elsewhere, Scripture uses the language of ordinary human life. By some process, the laws of which are at present unknown to us, but of which we get glimpses, in refraction, in the after-glow of sunset, in the fantastic appearances familiar to travelers in high latitudes and among the loftiest mountains—God was able to prolong the daylight until Israel had made an end of slaying their foes, with a very great slaughter, so that only a decimated remnant entered into the fenced cities. The how is not material to our present purpose. It is enough to express our belief in the fact itself. Somehow, the duration of that day's light was lengthened out until the people had avenged themselves of their enemies; "And there was no day like that before it or after it, that the Lord hearkened unto the voice of a man; for the Lord fought for Israel."

Our present purpose does not require us to follow the

steps of the conquerors as they passed from city to city. Some of them, like Lachish, seem to have made an obstinate resistance; others, like Hebron, must have been regarded with intense interest, because of their connection with the lives and wanderings of the patriarchs; others, again, witnessed to a high state of civilization, as Debir, the city of books and learning. All were treated with the same unsparing severity. The kings were slain, their bodies gibbeted till the evening; and all the souls smitten, so that none were left remaining—an utter destruction of all and every one by the edge of the sword.

We must remember that the Israelites were the executioners of divine justice, commissioned to give effect to the sentence which the foul impurities of Canaan called for. There is a judgment seat for nations as well as for individuals. Within the limits of the ages as they pass, and on the surface of this earth, that throne is erected and that judgment is proceeding. And the almighty Judge sees to it that his sentences are carried out. He has many agents—the Persian legions to execute his sentence on Babylon; the Vandals on Rome; the Russian Cossacks on Napoleon; as the Israelites on the Amorites, whose iniquity was now full, and threatened to infect the world.

4. THE LESSON FOR OUR OWN LIFE. There are days so extraordinary for the combination of difficult circumstances, human opposition, and spiritual conflict that they stand out in unique terror from the rest of our lives. Looking back on them, we may almost adopt the language of the sacred writer, "There was no day like that before it or after it."

But these days do not come, if we are living in fellowship with God, intent on doing his will, without there coming also his sweet "Fear them not; for I have delivered them into thy hands!" Our only anxiety should be that nothing divert us from his path, or intercept the communication of his grace. Like a wise commander, we must keep open the passage back to our base of operations, which is God. Careful about that, we need have no anxious care beside. The greatness of our difficulties is permitted to elicit the greatness of his grace. We may even be glad to enter the storm, that we may make fresh discoveries of the all-sufficiency of Jesus, who is never so near as in these days of special trial.

Moreover, these days may always be full of the realized presence of God. All through the conflict, Joshua's heart was in perpetual fellowship with the mighty Captain of the Lord's host, who rode beside him all the day. So amid all our conflicts, our hearts and minds should thither ascend, and there dwell where Christ is seated, drawing from him grace upon grace, as we need; like the diver on the ocean floor who, through his air hose, inhales the sustaining oxygen of the upper air. At these times it is very necessary not merely to ask God to help us, because the word *help* may mean that there is a great deal of reliance on self; and whatever there is of ourselves is almost certain to give way in the strain of battle. The divine part of our deliverance will be nullified by the alloy of our own energy, strength, or resolution. Let us substitute the word *keep* for the word *help*. Let us put the whole matter into the hands of God; asking him to go before us, to fight for us, to deliver us, as he did for his people on this eventful day.

In all such days we may have light which cannot be accounted for on any natural hypothesis. Our sun shall not go down, neither shall our moon withdraw itself; because the Lord shall be to us an everlasting light. Or in words spoken long after, which surely contain an allusion to this marvelous day of Gibeon, "It shall be one day which is known unto the Lord, not day and not night; but it shall come to pass that at evening time there shall be light" (Zech. 14:7, R.V.).

Only let us seek the grace of the Holy Spirit, that we may be kept in such an attitude of soul that we shall miss nothing of God's gracious and timely help. Trusting it, reckoning on it, appropriating it. Abiding in him, that we may ask with the certainty that God is hearkening unto the voice of man, and that he is fighting for us.

14

CLAIMING VICTORY

(JOSHUA 11)

"Up!—God has formed thee with a wiser view,
Not to be led in chains, but to subdue!
Calls thee to cope with enemies; and first
Points out a conflict with thyself—the worst!"
                                                    COWPER

THE Merom Waters, which must have become
encrimsoned with the blood of men on that great
day whose story we are now to tell, is described by
travelers as one of the fairest scenes in Palestine.

The lake is not large, but its blue waters are skimmed
by myriads of water fowl which make their home in the
forests of wavy reeds growing at the northern point
where the Jordan enters it. On the gentle undulation of
the hills that slope to it on the western side all the
episodes of pastoral life are transacted; while, from the
farther side, the gaunt hills, two miles across, frown
upon the placid scene.

To this sweet spot as mustering place, Jabin, King of
Hazor, aroused at last to fear and action by the tidings
of the day of Gibeon, summoned all the tribes of the
north of Canaan. Well would it have been for him—
speaking after the manner of men—if he had not delayed

so long, but had concentrated his forces in time to cooperate with Adonizedek, marching from the north simultaneously with the attack of the latter against Gibeon. To compensate for his lost opportunity, he now sent messengers with speed to raise the country. Possibly he adopted words like those with which, in after years, Saul summoned Israel to follow him to Jabesh-gilead, where he took a yoke of oxen and cut them in pieces, and sent them throughout all the borders of Israel, by the hand of messengers, saying, "Whosoever cometh not forth after Saul and after Samuel, so shall it be done unto his oxen."

Throughout the hills of Galilee the messengers sped— to the far north beneath the shadow of Lebanon, all down the Valley of Esdraelon to Carmel, and along the shores of the Great Sea. The Jebusite heard the summons in the hill country, and the Hivite under Hermon in the land of Mizpeh; and even some remnants of the shattered southern confederacy seem to have poured their scanty contribution into the accumulated ranks of that great host. "They went out, they and all their hosts with them, much people, even as the sand that is upon the seashore in multitude."

It was no time to dally in the camp at Gilgal, whither Joshua had led his warriors to refresh after their toils; and as soon as tidings reached him, he started with his army on the five days journey that intervened between Gilgal and Merom, and marched to perhaps the greatest battle of his life. Josephus tells us that the united forces consisted of 300,000 foot soldiers, 100,000 horsemen, and 20,000 chariots. He says also that the Israelites were terrified at having to encounter the iron chariots which drove swiftly into the ranks of an opposing army, enabling the warriors to discharge their missiles with terrible effect. It may be that some tidings of the immense array that lay waiting for him within the circle of the hills reached Joshua when he was within a day's march of the camp. A sense of the awfulness of the crisis may for a moment have thrilled his soul; but the steadfastness of his courage knew no shock, because, simultaneously with the tidings, there came the divine assurance, "Be not afraid because of them; for tomorrow about this time I will deliver them up all slain before Israel."

Joshua repeated the tactics which had been so successful previously. He came against them suddenly, perhaps in the early dawn. As the Israelites fell upon them, the vast host was seized with panic. Angel hosts, no doubt, cooperated from the heavenlies with the armies of the Lord; and the vaunted pride of the kings bit the dust as they beheld the awful rout that followed. Thousands must have fallen beneath the avenging sword; while three great bodies of fugitives made their way, one to the city of Sidon, forty miles distant; one to the seacoast, where in after years Elijah sojourned with the widow; one to Mizpeh, sheltering under Hermon.

The strength of the foe was broken; but for some years after this final victory Joshua carried on a campaign against the cities standing, each on its mound or hill (R.V.), according to the custom of the time, from which Jabin and his allies had sallied forth to fight. Hazor was burned, probably to intimidate the rest, being the most prominent in the alliance against Israel. For the rest, it was deemed sufficient to destroy the inhabitants that could bear arms, to render the horses useless, and to burn the chariots. "As the Lord commanded Moses his servant, so did Moses command Joshua, and so did Joshua; he left nothing undone of all that the Lord commanded Moses."

The Anakim warriors of extraordinary height, who had been the dread of Israel, were destroyed, together with their cities; and, nominally at least, the whole land passed into the hands of Israel.

1. IT WAS A DECISIVE VICTORY. Often before had the Canaanites rallied to oppose the progress of Israel;

but never after this did they dare to meet them in battle array. Their spirit was crushed, their power quelled. And herein we are reminded of the ascension of that greater Conqueror of whom Joshua was a type.

It is not improbable that those dark powers, who had opposed our Saviour throughout his earthly life, mustered for one last struggle as he left beneath his feet the cloud, bathed in the roseate light of dawn, that hid him from the eyes of his disciples. There is some trace of this in the words of the apostle, who tells us that he was raised far above all rule, and authority, and power, employing the very terms afterward used of our conflict with the wicked spirits in the heavenlies (Eph. 1:21; 6:12).

But in any case he triumphed over all that opposed him. "Having put off from himself the principalities and the powers, he made a show of them openly, triumphing over them." And the apostle, borrowing from one of the sublimest triumphal odes in the world, speaks of him as leading captivity captive (Col. 2:15, R.V.; Eph. 4:8).

Through the prophetess Deborah the Spirit of God first uttered that significant phrase when celebrating Israel's victory over a later Jabin, King of Hazor:

> "Arise, Barak, and lead thy captivity
>   captive,
> Thou son of Abinoam."*

The thought undoubtedly is that when the down-trodden becomes at last the victor, he leads captive that which had led him and others in captivity. The captive-making tyrant becomes in turn a captive.

So it was when Jesus rose and ascended into heaven. Up to that time Satan had usurped a supreme power over man; by the wiles of his temptations; by the witchery of the world; by the dread terrors of death and the grave; and by the virulence of his accusations. None had been

---

* Judges 5:12.

able to withstand him, and it seemed as if devil-power must be forever triumphant over man—over the strongest, as Samson; the wisest, as Solomon; the meekest, as Moses; the innocent, as Adam. But all this was reversed by the glorious deeds of our blessed Master, who, in his death, resurrection, and ascension defeated the devil, and demonstrated for evermore the supremacy of man in him over all the dark powers that infest the earth or air or heavenly places. "He led captivity captive." We can almost see the long line of princely captives following his triumphal chariot as he ascends—the world, which he had overcome; death, which he had abolished; Hades, the keys of which were wrenched from it to hang henceforth from his belt; the devil and his hosts; the principalities and powers of hell, led as a long line of slaves.

Never again need that conflict be repeated. It has been decisively demonstrated to the universe, and established forever, that though the first Adam was not able to withstand the assaults of the devil, but succumbed with all his race, yet the second Adam has proved himself more than conqueror; not for himself alone, but for all who are one with him by faith. There may be war in heaven; but it will largely resemble the warfare carried on by Joshua after his final victory—harassing and difficult, perhaps, but of no importance as affecting the result of the successes already gained. If Jesus vanquished the powers of darkness when they hurled themselves on him in the hour of his weakness and mortal agony, is it to be supposed for a moment that they will be able to effect anything now that he sits at the right hand of God, girded with power and glory?

2. THIS VICTORY NEEDED TO BE FOLLOWED UP AND APPROPRIATED. Though the victories of Israel were decisive, yet there was a sense in which they were incomplete. It is true that Joshua destroyed the cities and those whom he found in them; but it would seem that many of the inhabitants had previously retired for

safety to the rocky fastnesses or caves in the vicinity of their homes, so that as soon as the wave of conquest had passed over the land and subsided, they emerged from their hiding places, and reoccupied their possessions in houses and lands from which they had been temporarily dislodged. This was according to the word of Moses, who had predicted this very state of things when he said, "The Lord thy God will cast out those nations before thee by little and little; thou mayest not consume them at once, lest the beasts of the field increase upon thee" (Deut. 7:22).

It would have been in the highest degree impolitic to have exterminated all the inhabitants, for the land would have gone out of cultivation; the terraces, which were so needful in that hilly country, would have become broken down; and the water courses would have fallen hopelessly out of repair. And all this in addition to the reason alleged by the great lawgiver that the wild beasts would have multiplied to an alarming and dangerous extent. How much wiser, then, that the displacement of the Canaanites should be by a gradual process. The victories of Joshua were decisive, but they were not final. They needed to be followed up by the various tribes. There was no more doubt as to their success in prosecuting their victories than there had been in winning them. The one was as much guaranteed by the divine promise as the other. In the same breath as Moses had proclaimed the gradual process of Israel's settlement in the land of Canaan, he announced that the Lord their God would deliver their enemies up before them, discomfiting them with a great discomfiture till they were destroyed (Deut. 7:23).

The sacred historian even affirms that it was of the Lord to harden their hearts, to come against Israel in battle, that he might utterly destroy them (Josh. 11:20). We must not suppose, of course, that God stepped in to produce, in the case of these Canaanites, a result which would not have accrued to them by the working out of the natural laws which he has instituted. God loved them as he loves the world. They were included in the propitiation of Christ. They might have been saved, as Rahab was. And when it is said that God hardened their hearts, we must understand that their hearts became hardened by sinning against their light—in accordance with that great principle which God has established, that if a man resists his convictions of right he becomes more inveterate in his sinful ways. God is thus said to do what is done by the working out of the laws of that moral universe which he has constituted. It is clear that the Canaanites knew that God was with Israel. Rahab said, "I know that the Lord hath given you the land, and that your terror is fallen upon us, and that all the inhabitants of the land melt away before you. For we have heard, . . . and as soon as we had heard it, our hearts did melt; . . . for the Lord your God, he is God in heaven above, and on earth beneath" (Josh. 2:9–11). And the Gibeonites said, "We have heard the fame of the Lord, and all that he did in Egypt" (9:9–10). There is no doubt, then, that throughout the land there had gone forth the fame of God; and when the kings flung their hosts in battle against Israel it was as it has always been:

> "The kings of the earth set themselves,
> And the rulers take counsel together,
> Against the Lord, and against his
>   Anointed."

But how rich is the spiritual lesson to be derived from the peculiarity of this gradual appropriation of Joshua's achievements! "Joshua took the whole land, according to all that the Lord said unto Moses; and Joshua gave it for an inheritance unto Israel, according to their divisions by their tribes." Yet Israel had to fight over every inch of soil to drive out their conquered foes. So, as we have seen, our blessed Lord has won a decisive victory over all our foes; but we have to claim it repeatedly until, in the case of each of us, death, that last enemy, is destroyed.

The world is overcome; but we must overcome it by faith. The flesh has been nailed to the cross, and the old man has been done away; but we have by the Spirit to mortify the deeds of the body, that we may live. The devil has been vanquished once for all; but we have to hide ourselves in the Only-begotten, trusting him to keep us, so that the evil one may not touch us. The grave and death have been passed and left behind in the triumphal procession of the second Adam; but we must meet them, unless he come first, saying, as we approach them, "O death, where is thy sting? O grave, where is thy victory? Thanks be unto God, which giveth us the victory through our Lord Jesus Christ." We are more than conquerors in all things through him who loved us: but there never will be a day in our history when we shall not need to overcome by the word of our testimony and by the blood of the Lamb. Therefore the voice of the ascended Jesus speaks in sevenfold benediction to them that overcome.

There is no foe to your growth in grace, no enemy in your Christian work, no dreaded form of evil dominating and cursing the souls of men, which was not included in your Saviour's conquests. You need not be afraid of them. When you touch them, they will flee before you. God has promised to deliver them up before you. Only be strong and very courageous! Fear not, nor be dismayed! The Lord is with you, O mighty men of valor—mighty because one with the Mightiest. Claim victory! Whenever your enemies close in upon you, *claim victory!* Whenever heart and flesh fail, look up and CLAIM VICTORY! Be sure that you have a share in that triumph, which Jesus won not for himself alone, but for us all; remember that you were in him, when he won it—and *claim victory!* Reckon that it is yours, and gather spoil. Neither the Anakim nor fenced cities need daunt or abash you. You are one of the conquering legion. *Claim your share in the Saviour's victory.*

15

REST IN THE HEAVENLIES

(JOSHUA 11:23)

"He saw with Faith's far-reaching eye the fount
Of life, his Father's house, his Saviour God;
And borrowed thence to help his present want...
And so his eye upon the land of life
    He kept."

                                        POLLOK

T HE Book of Joshua naturally divides itself into two
    parts, the first of which deals with the conquest,
the second with the partition of the Land of Promise.
The junction of these two is at the close of the eleventh
chapter. There the story of the conquest ends, and that
of the partition begins. And just there we have the
significant record, "And the land had rest from war"—a
note of blessed tranquillity and peace, which is repeated
in the fourteenth chapter. But even that is not all; for in
the twenty-first chapter we are again told that "the Lord
gave Israel rest round about, according to all that he
sware unto their fathers."

Now, all this is in precise keeping with the spiritual
analogy that we have been tracing throughout this book;
and indeed the symbolism is so close that we are certain
that we are not following cunningly devised fables, but

are tracing the patterns of things in the heavens, sure anticipations of the plans and designs of God. He who embodied anticipations of Calvary in the sacrifices and offerings of Leviticus has embodied anticipations of the empty grave and the Ascension Mount in the conquest and apportionment of Canaan by Joshua. In the case of the glorious Antitype there was also a pause of blessed rest. Between the completion of his victory and the outpouring of the Holy Spirit, we are told that he sat down at the right hand of God. And in her noblest song the Church has repeatedly addressed him thus: "Thou sittest at the right hand of God, in the Glory of the Father."

The session of our Lord Jesus at the right hand of God is a graphic and beautiful metaphor, pregnant with food for holy thought. Obviously, it asserts the glorious honor of his majesty, that he is one with God in his divine nature. With equal clearness, it indicates the oneness of the Lord Jesus in the divine Unity of Being, albeit that he now wears our nature. But with similar force, it teaches us that he rests. The sitting posture naturally suggests repose. And we may reverently ask what was the nature of his rest, that we too may enjoy the Sabbath, which he keeps through the ages.

1. OUR SAVIOUR'S REST. It was not *the rest of overweariness.* When a man has wrought with vigor, he throws himself into a sitting posture to restore his exhausted energies. Now it is true that Jesus never spared himself. The intensity of his love and pity consumed prematurely the lantern in which they had been kindled. There had been the strain of unceasing toils, unsleeping vigils, and bitter sorrow; there had been the anguish of the Garden, and the weight of human sin; but none of these had availed to exhaust the divine energy of his being. On the morning of the resurrection he awoke, as a sleeper from refreshing slumber. He had not fainted, neither was he weary. And whatever else it meant, his session at the right hand of God did not imply that the

Saviour had overspent himself and needed rest.

Did it mean that he had entered on *a period of inaction,* and that there would be a pause put on his redemptive energies? The supposition has only to be stated to be dismissed. The evangelist Mark, who ends his Gospel on the high note of the Saviour's session at the right hand of God, instantly and in the same breath tells us that when his disciples went forth and preached everywhere, the Lord *worked* with them, and confirmed the word by the signs that followed. The descent of the Spirit at Pentecost, the government and maintenance of the Church, the perpetual communication of life and power from the Head to the members of his body, prove that behind the veil, which trembles as each spirit whom we have loved enters behind it, Jesus is at work. For Zion's sake he does not hold his peace, and for Jerusalem's sake he will not rest.

The rest of the Lord Jesus, symbolized by his session at God's right hand, was therefore not that of weakness or inactivity. What was it? Surely it meant that *he had finished* that which he rose up to do. He arose from the throne, emptied himself of his glory, stripped himself of much that was his by inherent right, and became flesh—that he might finish transgression, make an end of sins, make reconciliation for iniquity, and bring in everlasting righteousness. All these things he had done. On the cross he said, "It is finished"; from the throne he could say, "It is done." As it was said of Joshua, "He left nothing undone." And therefore, as the Father entered into his rest, when he had ceased from the work of creation—a rest, not of weariness or inactivity, but of a completed scheme—so did the Son enter into his rest when he ceased from laying the foundations, both of his redemptive work and of the future triumphs of his Church. Not weary; not inactive; but so far satisfied. He had done all that he essayed to do, all that could be done, and he sat down—the attitude of completion; of contentment; of calm expectancy for an inevitable result.

There is therefore great *doctrinal* significance in this vision of Christ, which perhaps has not been sufficiently considered. To quote words from the last charge of Dr. Wordsworth, the late lamented Bishop of St. Andrews, "It must, I am afraid, be said that the doctrine of Christ's session at the right hand of God, though stated plainly and repeatedly—not less than a dozen times—in the New Testament, and embodied in each of our three creeds, is not receiving from us the attention it deserves. It has been obscured by the undue prominence given to the doctrine of the other character in which he not only intercedes for us, but is supposed to be continually pleading in our behalf the merits of his precious death and sacrifice offered once for all upon the cross." And then he quotes with approval the words of the Liturgy, in reference to our Lord's sacrifice: "He is the very Paschal Lamb which *was offered* for us, and *hath taken away* the sin of the world."

When once the believer apprehends the meaning of the Lord's session at the right hand of God, he is not only assured of the divine majesty of Jesus, and of the Father's acceptance of his mediatorial work, but he goes further to realize that there is nothing to be added to that finished work. Since Jesus sits in the heavenly places, his sacrifice is sufficient and complete; his blood can avail for sins of crimson dye, and for a race of sinners; his obedience unto death has satisfied the demands of law, and its sword is sheathed; and through the universe, like a peal of marriage bells ringing in heaven, there goes the announcement that there is now no condemnation.

But there is an *experiential* significance also in the repeated affirmation of Scripture that our Lord sits at the right hand of God. We must never fail to bear in mind that the work of Jesus, since he took our nature into union with himself, is as the representative man.

As such he died, and rose, and reigns. And just in proportion as we are one with him by a living faith, we also shall die, and rise, and reign. Such thoughts were burning in the heart of the apostle when he said, "God raised us up with him, and made us to sit with him in the heavenly places in Christ Jesus" (R.V.). As the cathedral dome rears itself above the roar and strife, the smoke and mist, the slush and dirt of the streets—above the lounge of the idle, the hurry of the business-men, and the cry of the huckster and street urchin—so it is the purpose of God that we should sit with Christ and in Christ; that we should share in his triumph, his reign, and especially his rest; that we should drink deep draughts from the crystal depths of that river which washes the foot of the eternal throne.

2. IN WHAT RESPECT MAY WE SHARE CHRIST'S REST? It is a very needful question. Some of us have been men of war from our youth; we must see to it, lest, like David, we should be debarred from building the Temple of God. Only Solomons, whose names bespeak their peace, are competent for that. It is only when we are at rest that we can do our best work. It is said that it is impossible to get the highest results of workmanship when the workers are perturbed by the fever and rush of our modern life. The masterpieces of art come from days when the strain and pace were less, or from workshops where the roar of the tide is hardly heard, and the rush of life's hurricane is almost unperceived. So our best work for God cannot be done unless we have learned to be quiet; still, that God may mold us; tranquil, that the tremor of our nerves may not interfere with the thrill of his energy; calm, that we may drop the silt and mud, which make our hearts so dull and so inapt to mirror the deep blue of the heavens above.

The restful heart lives above the storm and strife, with Christ; sensitive to human sorrow and to its own, but able to discern the purposes of divine wisdom; to await the unfolding of the divine plan; and to trust the love of the divine heart. It keeps silence for his word. Its daily tasks are holy. It is not disturbed by emotional change. Such is its acquiescence in the divine will that it is content with whatever comes. Its winters are always going, its springs always coming; the turtledoves call softly within its woods, the flowers deck its soil. "I felt," said Fletcher, "the will of my God like unto a soft pillow, upon which I could lie down and find rest and safety in all circumstances."

There is no unnatural quietism in this life—rather the most intense earnestness and activity. When the nature is yielded up completely to the Holy Spirit, it attains to a speed of movement and a strength of endeavor which can only be accounted for by remembering that when once a man has surrendered himself to the current of the divine nature, he will acquire something of its velocity and force. But in the midst of the most rapid and vehement movement there is rest—deep rest, sweet rest.

There is *the rest of reconciliation.* The soul no longer works up toward the cross to obtain justification. It is assured that all that needed to be done to win it had been done when Jesus said, "It is finished." Thus standing at the foot of the cross, conscious of his acceptance through the precious blood, the redeemed sinner cries, "Who shall lay anything to the charge of God's elect?" And he does not wait for a counter-challenge, because he is so sure that there can be none.

There is *the rest of assured victory.* Before we understand the meaning of our Lord's ascension, we oppose Satan by the armory of our own resolves and efforts at amendment. We fight and strive, and vow and fail, and start again. But when we realize all that Jesus has done, we come to see that Satan is a conquered foe; that his weapons cannot reach a life hidden with Christ in God; and that so long as we maintain our standing in our risen Lord, we need not dread his attacks, nor be perturbed in the affray.

There is *the rest of a surrendered will.* When our wills move off the pivot of self on to the pivot of God, then our lives become concentric with the life of God; our hearts are allured to his love, our feet keep step to the marching music of his divine purpose. Oh, the bliss of living when our wills blend with his, like perfect words married to perfect music! Then trial and sorrow are treated as our Father's messengers, but in their winter costume. Then our very infirmities indicate the direction into which we should send our energies. Then disappointment becomes impossible, because all is God-appointed. Then we always have our way, because God's and ours are one. Then prayer is the discovery of God's plans, and a taking hold of his willingness. Then the heart keeps Sabbath, like a valley encircled by the great mountains on which the storms expend themselves.

There is *the rest of unbroken fellowship.* For as Jesus is one with the Father, so we become one with him, and through him one with the Blessed Trinity, according to his own prayer: "I in them, and Thou in Me, that they may be made perfect in one." What pen can describe the blessed fellowship between the Father, the Son, and the Holy Spirit, in the serene tranquillity of the divine nature? Yet something of that may be realized by those who claim that they shall be admitted to enjoy all that Jesus has purchased for his Church.

There is *the rest of perfect love.* Our affections have sorely troubled us, straying far away to forbidden things, and allying us to many drifting islets, lovely to the eye, but unstable as the tide. But when we enter into the life of the Ascended Jesus—which is the life of Pentecost— we find that our hearts become pervaded by the love of God. There is no longer the murmur of the babbling brook; because the great ocean has poured its waters up, filling its bed. There is no longer the yearning and jealousy and bitterness of unsatisfied desire; because the heart has found in God all its desires more than met. It hungers no more, neither thirsts any more; for the Lamb who is in the midst of the throne satisfies it with the green pastures and still waters of eternal love. It is silent in its love.

There is also *the rest of the holy heart*. It is not occupied with inbred lust, not tossed to and fro on seething passion, or driven by every gusty whim. The flesh is crucified, the self-principle is quelled, the empire of the Holy Saviour is supreme. Emmanuel has taken the throne, and all discordant elements are still.

It may be that some who read these lines are passing through great suffering, and in that suffering are tempted to feverish restlessness. They expend themselves as the imprisoned songster from the woods that beats itself passionately against its cage bars. It is almost useless to bid such to rest and be still. They must learn the source of rest. Let them see that Jesus has entered into his rest that they might enter it too. Let them open their hearts for him to breathe in his gentle resurrection message, "Peace be unto you." Let them reverently and believingly claim this also as part of their inheritance, of which they are co-heirs with Christ.

3. HOW TO ENJOY THIS REST. But these blessed experiences are only possible through the power of the Holy Spirit. The ascension of Jesus is mystically and inevitably connected with the descent of the Holy Spirit. As the one Advocate passed up into the glory, the other came down into the heart of the Church, that he might realize in our experience that which is ours in the purpose and intention of God, creating within us the faith that shall be able to claim our share in that inheritance of rest which Christ has won for us. You cannot divorce these two thoughts; or, if you do, you will bring inevitable disappointment into human hearts. If you magnify your rights in the glorified Saviour, and fail to unfold the willingness of the Holy Spirit to make them

your own in daily and living enjoyment, you set souls the impossible task of climbing inaccessible heights, and they abandon hope. Or, if you always dwell on the Pentecostal fullness, apart from the Saviour, whom the Holy Spirit has come to glorify, you drive souls into a self-analysis, an introspection, a spiritual self-centeredness, which is fatal to their true development. Teach men the meaning of Christ's session, and that they have a right to all it means of the rest of God; but tell them also that the power to claim that right is through the grace of the Holy Spirit, whom God has given to those who obey him.

We must not anticipate the teaching of the remaining chapters. For what student of the analogies of this wonderful book can doubt that "the much land to be possessed" of the following chapters refers to the gracious fullness of the Holy Spirit which awaits our quest? But as we close this meditation on the rest that awaits all the people of God who sit with Christ in the heavenly places, let us lift our hearts to the Blessed Spirit, asking that he would reveal to us that which eye has not seen, nor ear heard, nor the heart of man conceived, but which God has prepared for those who love him.

16

LAND TO BE POSSESSED

(JOSHUA 13:1)

"Then be it so!
For in better things we yet may grow;
Onward and upward still our way,
With the joy of progress from day to day;
Nearer and nearer every year
To the visions and hopes most true and dear."
                                    F. R. HAVERGAL

JOSHUA was probably about ninety years of age when the conquest of Canaan was complete. But a very important part of his work had yet to be performed. It would not have been enough for him to have asserted Israel's supremacy over the Canaanites unless he had taken measures to follow up his victories by settling the people in their stead. The work of destruction must be succeeded by that of construction. The warrior must give place to the administrator and statesman.

The first step toward the occupation of Canaan was taken in the summons of the Lord to his servant, who had so faithfully performed all his word. Though he was old and well stricken in years, he was still the confidant of Jehovah, the depositary of his secrets, the executor of his plans. To bear fruit in old age, to put forth leaves and fruit amid the decay of physical vigor, to sweep on from the rapids of youth to the deep water of the river's mouth with ever increasing fullness and abundance; to be as able to build up the people of God in the golden autumn as to lead them to victory in the early spring—this is no common honor, no ordinary achievement. And it was a high tribute to Joshua that when he had overstepped the ordinary limit of human life by twenty years, he was summoned to put the crown on the work of his life.

The method adopted seems to have been, first, a careful survey of the land not yet possessed; then, its apportionment among the several tribes according to their size; and lastly, the actual appropriation and acquisition of each portion by the efforts of the tribe to which it was assigned. It is with the first of these that we have now to deal. After the divine voice had summoned the veteran leader to the last great work of his life, it proceeded to enumerate the portions of land that yet remained; and some time after, when seven of the tribes were as yet unsettled and there was urgent need for the completion of the task, twenty-one commissioners were appointed to pass through the land and examine it, and make a report concerning it to Joshua at Shiloh.

It would be interesting, did space permit, to examine the area designated by the divine Spirit. This at least we must notice as we pass, that it included all the region of Philistia, inhabited by some of the stoutest foes that Israel ever encountered, and who were a perpetual source of weakness and danger till the times of the kings. There were also the rich pasture lands of the south; and in addition the luxuriant plain of Phoenicia and the fertile upland valleys, cooled by the snow-capped summits and watered from the rivulets of Lebanon—all portions of the land on which Israel had always a very slender hold. Compare this outline sketch of the divine intentions with the territories then actually held and afterward possessed by Israel, and the difference between God's ideal and their real inheritance becomes very striking.

The same appalling contrast appears when we recall the original promise made to Joshua at the beginning of this book. "From the wilderness and this Lebanon, even unto the great river, the river Euphrates, all the land of the Hittites, and unto the Great Sea toward the going down of the sun, shall be your border" (R.V.). Yet, as a matter of fact, Israel filled up the measure of this prediction for once only, and for a very short time, during its tenure of Canaan. Solomon did for a brief space realize the divine ideal; but the radiant glory of his kingdom was soon hemmed in and obscured by the clouds that drew up their dark veils over the sky. Men have sometimes used this as an argument against the divine veracity. It should rather be quoted as a melancholy confession of human frailty, and of failure to claim and appropriate the promises of God. There is no variableness in God. It is impossible even for our unbelief to make his promises of none effect.

Let us consider whether there may not be a similar contrast between that which God has intended for us and that which we have made our own. Spread out in the Bible, and set forth in the life of Jesus, there is for us, as for Joshua, a map of what God desires for his people. Here, as in a divine Doomsday Book, is a list of the mountains of vision and the valleys of blessing; of the green pasturelands and the waters of rest; of the cities we may occupy and the foes we may expel. All is mapped out for us; and we shall do wisely to carefully ponder it, that we may be humbled as we see the slow progress we have made, and may be stirred up to apprehend all that for which we were apprehended in Christ Jesus.

1. IN THE DIRECTION OF KNOWLEDGE. We must distinguish between intellectualism and knowledge. It is not so difficult to acquire the former, with all those

aids for acquiring information which abound around us. The very newspaper press, awaking to discover that man has other needs than those of the politician, is beginning to bring the discoveries of science and the contents of books to our breakfast tables. Leisure and taste, memory and mental discipline, observation and society will do a good deal toward imparting that strange veneer called *culture;* but this is a very different thing from *knowledge.* A man may be utterly destitute of culture and yet may have that direct and intuitive perception of truth which as much surpasses it as the blue of heaven does the painted scenery of a theater. Whereas a man may be quick, clever, intellectual, well-informed, and able to lay his hands readily on his information, and yet be utterly destitute of the true knowledge.

God meant us to know himself even as Jesus knew him, in his human life. Remember how often he said, *I know him.* No mist ever crept up between the outspread landscape of God's nature and the loving, ravished gaze that swept over it; passing from the high mountains of his righteousness to the great sea of his judgments, and dwelling with rapture on the verdant tracts of his love and pity and grace—on the mighty rivers that represent the fertilizing out-goings of his being, and on the wealth of that blessed existence, like a summer-land, every inch of which is full of ripening fruit. Such knowledge, high and wonderful though it be, and unattainable by our own endeavors, is brought within our reach by our blessed Lord. He gives us eternal life in order that we might know the only true God. He bids us stand on Calvary that we may behold the heart of the Father. He reveals God to us in his own life, so that to know him is to know God. And yet how little do we know the Father! We know little about him, and less of him by personal intimacy and fellowship.

To take the lowest test, *our knowledge of God's Word.* While some individual explorers have pressed on into unknown and untrodden lands, the large majority of professing Christians are content with a few familiar and well-trodden patches. They read and read again the same passages in the Gospels, the Psalms, or Isaiah; but they never venture into the unexplored territory beyond. And the saddest point of all is that they have no deeper perception of the words which have become so familiar to them than at the first. They are like the busy crowds which pass lightly over the graves of martyrs, obliterating the sacred inscriptions, and missing the deeper thoughts which crowd in on the historian who bends over them in reverent meditation.

There are many subjects which the bulk of Christian people, by a tacit understanding, refuse to enter. Such are, among others, the Second Advent; the Restoration of Israel, and its future mission to mankind; the great question of fulfilled and unfulfilled prophecy; the mystical union of Christ with those who believe in him. In all these respects there is much land to be possessed. Well may we be rebuked by the example of the Psalmist, who took days and nights to master his scanty and meager Bible! We have much to learn from Nehemiah and many other characters in Holy Writ, whose prayers and songs are little else than chains of scriptural quotations. Let us mend our ways, not always traverse the well-trodden paths, but seek for a completer acquaintance with the entire range of truth as given in God's Word.

And if we know comparatively little of the Bible, we know less of God. Some of us dwell on one trait of his character, in complete ignorance of others. We magnify his mercy at the expense of his righteousness; or his justice at the cost of his grace. Our knowledge of him, moreover, is borrowed from hearsay evidence, and from the reports of others. We do not hear and know him for ourselves. We are not content to know at second hand the symphonies of Beethoven or the pictures of Murillo. And we ought not to rest content till we can say with the patriarch, "I have heard of thee with the hearing of the ear, but now mine eye seeth thee." Oh to know God, to follow on to know him, until he break on our hearts as the morning or as the early rain! What ecstasy there is in discovering new traits of character, new beauties in our friends, as we come across some undreamed-of excellence! So there would be a new meaning in life if we began to explore what is to many of us a *terra incognita*, the Being of God. There is much land here to be possessed.

2. IN THE DIRECTION OF CHRISTIAN ATTAINMENT. In us, as in Canaan of old, there are the seven nations of sin. Hereditary tendencies to evil; unholy habits that have intrenched and fortified themselves; worldly compliances which have become part of our existence. When first we became Christians we made a determined onslaught on these things, and met with much success; but we have become weary of incessant watchfulness and conflict. We have no taste for the girt loin and the erect, alert, soldier attitude. Our heart is only touched here and there by Christ; and our peace is incessantly broken by the raids of those unextirpated evils, which swoop down from time to time, carrying everything before them. There is much land still to be possessed.

Would it not be well to enumerate the points in which we are deficient—not in a spirit of morbid self-scrutiny, but of honest self-analysis? Is not the first step toward an amended life a clear appreciation of what needs amending? We may well turn from our own efforts at self-knowledge and bare our hearts to the inspection of the Spirit of God, asking him to search us and show us what wicked way there is in us before he leads us in the way everlasting.

In some cases it is the business life, the workshop, or the counting-house which is not possessed by Christ, and is kept altogether and constantly outside the range of his influence. In other cases it is the social element, or the home relationships of our nature which are not brought into captivity to him. The spirit is yielded, but not the soul; or the soul, but not the body. We accept God's reign over the principal departments of our being; but there are certain outstanding habits over which we are reluctant to admit his sway.

Consider how great is God's ideal for each of us. To be "conformed to the image of his Son"! Scan his fair proportions; his strength and sweetness; his holiness and pity; his hatred of sin and love to the sinner; his devotion to God; his life of self-sacrifice for man. Is that God's ideal? And does he predestinate each of us to be conformed to it? Then who of us need renounce hope? But ah, how much there is to be possessed! How little do we possess of his beauty or strength or tenderness or holiness!

The soul is first possessed by Christ, and then it begins to possess Christ. We are apprehended by our divine Captor, and then we come to apprehend him. We open our hearts to receive him into their depths, and then learn to appropriate him by a living faith. In other words, consecration must precede appropriation. But when once the act of consecration is complete, we may begin to possess him. This blessed habit may be initiated in a single act; but it is built up by a series of such acts, which are maintained, through the grace of the Holy Spirit, till it becomes as natural for us to look up to Jesus and to claim whatever we need as to breathe. Ah, soul, why pine in poverty and starvation? Is it not because you have withheld yourself from Jesus? Arise, and yield yourself to him! Let him possess you; and then you may claim a reciprocal possession of your Lord. Thus shall you begin to enter upon your eternal inheritance, and commence to expend yourself on pursuits that shall engage you when sun and moon are no more!

3. IN THE DIRECTION OF THE GIFTS OF THE HOLY SPIRIT. "To each one of us is given grace according to the measure of the gift of Christ" (Eph. 4:7, R.V.). And

the context clearly shows that this is not the common grace needed for daily living but the special gifts of grace of the Pentecostal fullness of the Holy Spirit, acquired for us by the ascended Lord. If we understand the teaching of the Epistles aright, there is for each member of the mystical body of Christ a distinct share in the Pentecostal gift. We may describe it as a share in his baptism or in his fullness. This is immaterial. But there is surely something more than is ordinarily understood by regeneration, or the gift of faith, or the revelation of the living Saviour. There is a power, an overflowing love, an assurance, an exuberant joy, a freedom, which are not enjoyed by all Christians but which are as evidently their birthright as they are to be desired.

And, in addition, there are the bestowments of the Holy Spirit, by which we are specially qualified to do Christ's work in the world. Tact in leadership; wisdom to win souls; power to help believers into a fuller life; utility to administer, or to speak, or to teach; sympathy, facility in utterance, power in prayer. These may be named among others. The whole continent of Pentecostal blessing is avoided by many believers as if it were full of swamps, of fever, noisome pestilence; it stands upon their globes as Africa did in the days of our childhood. There is surely in this direction much land to be possessed.

But oh, let us not be content simply to know our failures and deficiencies! Let us arise and quit ourselves like men. Let us ask our heavenly Joshua to settle us in this good land; so that there may be no rill or valley or mountain or tract of territory unpossessed. God has given us in Christ all things which pertain unto life and godliness; let us claim the whole of our inheritance by a living faith, so that we may enter on the enjoyment of all that is possible for us on this side of heaven.

17

A VETERAN COMRADE

(JOSHUA 14 AND 15)

"Simple lives, complete and without flaw . . .
Who said not to the Lord as if afraid,
'Here is thy talent in a napkin laid,'
But labored in their sphere, as those who live
In the delight that work alone can give."
LONGFELLOW

IT was in Gilgal that the apportionment of Canaan took place. There, where the reproach of Egypt had been rolled away, and where the main camp had stood—gathered around the Tabernacle during the years that the warriors had been afar from wives and children, fighting the battles of Jehovah—it was fit that the rewards of victory should be meted out. It was a great epoch in Israelite story, as the tribes assembled around their veteran leader, before whom and Eleazar stood the urns, the one containing the name of each, and the other the name of some specified portion of that fair land, which lay all around, smiling from hills and vales to the blue heaven above.

Judah, first in war and march, was the first to draw nigh. It was a great people, and was destined yet to play a greater part in the history of Israel and of mankind.

But an incident intercepted the casting of the lot which calls for earnest heed; for, after all, our religious life is a thing for ourselves, and we learn more from the act and word of individuals than from the movement of a tribe. Stand still, then, O Christian soul, and see some counterpart of yourself in your best moments, in this demand of the gray-headed warrior, this lion's whelp, for that is the underlying thought in the name "Caleb." Strong, bold, heroic, there was a great deal of the lion in him beside his name. He had been the young lion of the tribe of Judah some fifty years before; but he was as strong as he stepped out of the ranks of Judah to claim his right as he was when Moses sent him to spy out the land.

1. THE PRIME CHARACTERISTIC OF CALEB'S EARLY LIFE HAD BEEN HIS ENTIRE DEVOTION TO GOD. Repeatedly we are told both of him and Joshua that they "wholly followed the Lord." And there was some trace of this in the words of the old man, as he addressed the comrade of many a hard-fought fight, of many a weary march. The rest of the spies had turned aside, dismayed by the spectacle of giants and walled-up cities and vast battle array. They had ceased to keep the eye steadfastly fixed on the movements of God's will, and on the might of his hand; and instead of following hard after him, they had yielded to panic, and made the hearts of the people melt.

But there had been no panic in the heart of Caleb. He had only been considering that, when God delights in men, he brings them into the land of milk and honey, and makes it theirs by deed of gift. And as he thought in his heart, so he spake with his mouth. In his rough soldier's phrase he even dared to boast that the Canaanites were but bread waiting to be eaten by the hosts of Israel. And then in more thoughtful fashion he spoke of the shadow of God's protection as having passed from over the land, as if he had the consciousness of it being deserted by God.

He followed God wholly through the weary years that ensued. Amid the marchings and counter-marchings, the innumerable deaths, the murmurings and rebellions of the people, he retained a steadfast purpose to do only God's will, to please him, to know no other leader, and to heed no other voice. It was of no use to try and involve that stout lion's cub in any movement against Moses and Aaron. He would be no party to Miriam's jealous spite. He would not be allured by the wiles of the girls of Moab. Always strong and true and pure and noble; like a rock in a changeful sea, like a snow-capped peak in a change of cloud and storm and sun. A man in whose strong nature weaker men could hide, and who must have been a tower of strength to that new and young generation which grew up to fill the vacant places in the van of Israel. The Nestor of the Hebrew camp, in him the words of the Psalmist were anticipated: he bore fruit in old age, and to the last was fat and flourishing.

And two things lit the path of this Great-heart, 'mid the gloom of the wanderings and the chaos of the conquest. There was, first, the consciousness that lay upon his heart, like sunshine on a summer ocean, that God delighted in him; that the outgoings of God's nature toward him were full of love and joy; and that the peace of God that passes all understanding might be his inalienable possession. Walking in the light, as God was in the light, he had fellowship with God; and he bore with him the rest of the divine nature long before he entered into its transitory type in the Land of Promise.

There was, next, the thought of Hebron. Forty-five years had passed since he had seen the white buildings of that ancient and holy city nestling beneath its terebinths. Probably he had only dwelt there for a single hour or two, while his comrades were bartering for pomegranates and oranges and the rich produce of its vales and hills; but it left an ineffaceable impression upon his heart. He had seen the Vale of Eshcol where they cut down the bunch of grapes; but it had no attractions to him compared to the city on which he had fixed his desire. He had beheld Jerusalem, beautiful for situation and girdled by its mountains; but to his lover's eye it had no glory by reason of that greater glory that excelled. And even the Plain of Esdraelon, watered by the Kishon brook, could not steal away his fond attachment to Hebron. Hebron, beneath whose oaks Abraham had pitched his tent; Hebron, whose soil had been trodden by the feet of the Incarnate God, as with two angel attendants he visited the tent of Abraham; Hebron, where Sarah and Abraham, Isaac and Rebekah, Jacob and Leah, lay buried, each in a little niche, holding the land in trust, as the graves of the dead always hold the land for the living, until the promise of God was realized, and the seed of Abraham could return to claim its heritage.

God had read his secret, and had arranged that what his heart loved best his hand should take, and hold, and keep. It was one of the things which God had himself prepared for those who love him. He had taught him to love it, and immediately on his return to the camp the divine order was promulgated, "My servant Caleb, because he hath another spirit with him, and hath followed me fully, him I will bring into the land whereinto he went, and his seed shall possess it." That promise fell into his heart as water on a thirsty soil, or like a lover's last word cherished through long years. Often, as he lay down to sleep beside the campfire, his last thought would be of Hebron; and amid the noontide haze, when the mirage gleamed on the horizon, it would sometimes seem to him as if the green hills of Hebron were beckoning him across the waste. What though his comrades were carried out to die day after day—plague could not touch him, pestilence could not harm him, and death itself must drop the point of its spear when it came near his heart.

We have trace of the attitude of Caleb's heart through

those long years in the words he spoke at this memorable juncture, when he said: "Behold, the Lord hath kept me alive, as he said. . . . Now therefore give me this mountain, whereof the Lord spake in that day; . . . as the Lord said." The promise of God was his stay and comfort and exceeding great reward. He had to wait for its fulfillment, and it seemed long; as waiting times always do, especially when man waits for God. But God was working for him while he was waiting (Isa. 64:4, R.V.).

2. SUCH DEVOTION AS CALEB'S HAS MARVELOUS RESULTS.

(a) *It is the soil from which such a faith springs as can claim the realization of promise.* "Now therefore give me this mountain, whereof the Lord spake in that day." No common faith was needed to make so large a claim. Think of the time that had elapsed! Think of the greatness of the bequest, such a possession! Think of the Anakim that held it in their giant hands! But faith triumphed. And if the words "It may be" came into his speech, words with a falter in them, the tremor, as it were, of fear, we must understand that they did not spring from any doubt of God, but of that mistrust of self which is a trait in all moral greatness. No man of noblest mold is ever self-confident. While he reckons infinitely on God, he always answers the charge of impending treachery with the whisper, "Lord, is it I?"

The weakness of your faith is due, not to any inherent incapacity for faith, but because you have not yet learned the meaning of the words "He wholly followed the Lord his God." There is waiting for you an inheritance—some promised Hebron, some blessed gift of God's infinite love in Christ. It is for you to say, with the faith of a Caleb, "Give me this mountain."

(b) *It leads to fellowship.* Hebron stands for friendship, fellowship, love. The old word means that; and perhaps that is why Caleb was so eager to strike out the recent giants' name of Kirjath-arba (Josh. 14:15), and to bring back the word that Abraham had often had upon his lips. It spoke to him of that communion with his unseen Friend that he had enjoyed through the wanderings and vicissitudes of his long life, and which was not to end now; because in the seclusion of his estate, beneath the shadow of his own vine and fig tree, he would speak with him as a man with his friend, and anticipate the experiences of Nathanael in the days when the Gospel walked incarnate on our earth.

So is it ever. You must give yourself away to God, and follow him, as the novice in Alpine climbing does his guide, or you will never be able to live in the Hebron where God gives himself to the soul in passages of love which it is not lawful for man to utter. "If any man love me, he will keep my word; and my Father will love him, and we will come to him and make our abode with him." The world wants love. It is full of tired faces, and aching limbs, and breaking hearts. Only through man does the love of God come to men. This is the reason that the Word became flesh, so that God might be able to pour the full exuberance of his love not only *over* them, as in sunshine and fruitful seasons, but *into* them. And now redeemed men who are one with the divine Man must through him become the channels by which that blessed love may flow. But if any of us aspire to this, he must take up his abode in Hebron, to leave it never. His must be its balmy air, its terraced slopes, its sunny warmth. Like the beloved apostle—whose first epistle might fairly have been dated from the sweet calm of Hebron rather than from the strife of the heathen Ephesus—we must live in the love of God. His love must dwell unhindered in us. But the only gateway into such an experience is the obedience that counts not cost, and makes no exceptions, but follows fully its highest convictions of the will and law of God.

Those who follow God know God. He turns and sees them following, and hears their inquiry to know his secret place, and bids them "come and see." Oh, bliss of bliss! They tarry with him in such friendship as Moses had on the Mount. Their hearts burn and glow as the hours pass by unheeded, uncounted. They come forth with the light of love transfiguring their faces, and making their common dress shine with lustrous beauty, as though they, too, had made light their vesture.

(c) *It leads to strength.* "Lo," said Caleb. "I am this day fourscore and five years old. As yet I am as strong this day as I was in the day that Moses sent me; as my strength was then, even so is my strength now for war, both to go out and to come in." Consecration is the source of undecaying strength, because it allows the soul to draw on the strength of God. Just as the sap flows through the tender vine branches in spring, so does the strength of God pass into those that believe; who are not only united to him, but fully surrendered and given up to his indwelling.

It is this point that Isaiah emphasizes in his sublime contrast between the respective strength of youth and of those that wait on Jehovah. He says that under circumstances that sap the vigor of early manhood, so that youths faint and are weary, and young men utterly fail, those "that wait on the Lord renew their strength. They mount up . . . they run . . . they walk." It is the last of these that is so difficult. It is not so difficult *to soar.* When the day is young, and the deep blue heavens tempt the exploring wing, and the breeze is soft, it is hard to linger by the few twigs on the top of the bare rocks. It is not very difficult *to run.* When the sunbeams are still aslant, and the dew has not left the grass, and the dust is not stirred, there is a feeling of exhilaration which compels us to substitute our quickest pace for the more sedate walk. But *to walk!* To go forward in the sultry heat! To have patience, and bear for his name's sake, and not grow weary! To resist the temptation to lethargy and indolence and luxurious ease! This is the greatest task of all! But for this, which had been Caleb's experience for forty-five years of desert wandering, no human energy can suffice. The soul must learn to take the power which God gives to the faint; and to receive the strength he increases to such as have no might.

But this strength is accessible only through obedience. God cannot and will not bestow it except where there is a thoughtful and deliberate purpose to do his will, to follow his path, and to execute his work. But if you are set on this, then adequate strength for body and soul, mind and heart, will and spirit, shall most certainly be forthcoming. The outward man may decay; but the inward man will be renewed day by day.

(d) *It gives victory.* Of all the Israelites that received their inheritance in the Land of Promise, Caleb appears to have been the only one who succeeded in perfectly expelling the native occupiers of the country. The Israelites generally seem to have made but poor headway against their strong and mighty foes, with their chariots of iron and fenced walls. Repeatedly we encounter the sorrowful affirmation, *they were not able to drive them out.* But Caleb was a notable exception. Arba was the greatest man among the Anakim (Josh. 14:15); his three grandsons, Sheshai and Ahiman and Talmai, the sons of Anak, were prepared to yield their lives rather than give up possession (15:14)! Yet Caleb drove them out—not he indeed, but the Lord, who was with him, and gave him a victory that must have otherwise eluded even his strong hands. The man who wholly followed the Lord was alone wholly victorious.

How precious and searching is the conclusion! Our failures in expelling the giants of the heart, in dealing with inbred corruption and the assaults of Satan, are almost entirely due to some failure in consecration. We have not wholly followed the Lord. There has been some secret flaw, some leakage, some draining away of strength. This must be put right before the other can be secured. But when, so far as we know, we are entirely yielded to God, then no sin can stand before us, because nothing can stand before him. We humbly and trustfully put the matter into his hands, and believe that he will go forth against our foes in the chariots of salvation.

(e) *It enables us to give blessings to others.* Twice we are told how Achsah, Caleb's daughter—who was such a lovely prize, fit to repay Othniel for his risk of life in taking Debir, the city of the books—lighted down from her ass to ask a blessing from her father's hands. As dowry he had given her a field that lay toward the south, but which was destitute of springs. To water it entailed the conducting of irrigating streams from a distance. The newly married pair talked over the matter between themselves, and felt how desirable it was to be possessed of springs; and as Othniel shrank from asking, she took it on herself to obtain the boon from Caleb. "Give me also springs of water. And he gave her the upper and the nether springs."

In the Epistle to the Galatians the apostle speaks of men who supplied or ministered the Spirit to them (3:5). It is a remarkable expression, as though through the "hearing of faith" men were able to become channels through which the Spirit was supplied to others. What a marvelous power! Is this the spiritual reality of which the laying on of hands was the sacrament and sign? May we say that even now there is a spiritual contact with men and women who are living in the Hebron of fellowship, through which the upper and nether springs of spiritual grace are communicated?

Follow the Lord fully. Then will you dwell in the land. Then will your heart become as a watered garden, and a spring of water that does not fail. Then will you be able to obtain promises, not for yourself only, but for others. Then shall rivers of living water flow through you, and those who know you best. The Othniels and Achsahs of your home circle will gather round you to ask a blessing, and you shall have power to open springs of spiritual blessing in the heights of the heavenly places, and in the depths of daily practical ministry, in the valley of human life.

18

RECEIVING AND REIGNING

(ROMANS 5:17)

"Each holy purpose help us to fulfill!
Increase our faith to feed upon thee still!
Illuminate our minds, that we may see
All around us holy signs of thee.
And may such witness in our lives appear,
That all may know thou hast been with us here!"
BOURNE

THE allotment of Canaan, which was inaugurated beneath the direction of Joshua and Eleazar in Gilgal, and had been temporarily arrested by the claim of Caleb, now proceeded. And, in the first instance, the three great tribes of Judah, Ephraim, and Manasseh received their inheritance. Half the tribe of Manasseh had already received its lot, given by Moses on the farther side of the Jordan. And therefore the descendants of Joseph, in the first instance, received but one lot, and cities were separated for the children of Ephraim in the midst of the inheritance of the children of Manasseh (Josh. 16:9; 17:14).

The limits of these great tribes are carefully mentioned. That of Judah in the fifteenth chapter, even to its uttermost cities. That of the children of Joseph in the sixteenth and seventeenth. From this we may infer that there is a specific share in the gifts of the ascended Saviour for each of us; just as there is a specific work to be done by each in the building of the Church and the ingathering of men. "*Unto every one of us* is given grace, according to the measure of the gift of Christ" (Eph. 4:7). And again, *to each one* is given the manifestation of the Spirit to profit withal. That there should be diversities of gifts and workings and ministrations is not to be wondered at. This is in harmony with the constitution of the human mind, which in no two persons is alike. But though the talents assigned to each vary in the same way that natural ability does, yet no one of the King's servants is left without some precious deposit. Not all have five talents; but each has one. For each there is a piece of wall to build, a corner in the vineyard, a place in the ranks of temple service; and for each there is a store of special grace and gift, won by the risen Lord, and awaiting bestowment from his hands.

Concerning each of these tribes, there is made the same melancholy confession which is heard repeatedly in this and the following book, like the monotonous note of a storm-bell rung by the wild waves on a dangerous coast: "They could not drive them out." "But the Canaanites would dwell in that land" (17:12).

Mark the strength of that word *would*. It was no expression for those Canaanites to use. They were a dispossessed race. They had neither part nor lot in Canaan; and Israel made a profound mistake in allowing them to remain in the face of God's great word, "I will drive them out from before the children of Israel"—yet let us not condemn them, lest we condemn ourselves. There is not the least reason why besetting sin or fleshly lusts should hold their own, or find any foothold in the region of the saved nature. Never allow them to say *they must* or *they will.* Granted that they would be able to keep us at bay, they have no weight in the presence of that Omnipotence which vanquished them on the cross, and is pledged to destroy them utterly.

The presence of the Canaanites led to an altercation between the children of Joseph and Joshua. "Why hast thou given me but one lot and one part for an inheritance, seeing I am a great people?" (R.V.). Like so many more, they were content to live on the strength of past tradition, upon their numbers and prestige; and to base upon these considerations claims which they were too indolent to make good by deeds.

"If you are a great people," Joshua replied, "there is plenty of unoccupied territory within the limits of your inheritance. Forest land perhaps! There fell trees, extract the stumps, and grow crops upon the rich and verdant soil fertilized by the leaves of many autumns." How often we ask God for wider spheres of usefulness, while we fail to utilize those which lie within our reach. "Cut down the woods," is an injunction which might very fairly apply to us all. Do not sigh for missionary service till you have covered the whole acreage within your reach—in the home circle, or among the children of some poor district. The woods may be thick, but the axe of persevering faith will make a clearing there.

"The hill country," persisted they, "is not sufficient, and the valley is filled by Canaanites with their iron chariots; give us more."

"No," said Joshua. "You have power enough to cut down the woods, and to drive out the Canaanites—use it." For all the territory which we should win for God we have sufficient power, if we would but use it; there is no work so hard, no temptation so mighty, no post so difficult, but there is also sufficient grace contained within the one great gift of the Holy Spirit to meet our every requirement. Perhaps the best path to the speedy acquisition of spiritual power, for the majority of those who shall read these lines, would be to claim and use the abundance of grace which is within their reach awaiting them in the living Saviour.

This brings us out upon the text that stands at the head of this chapter, which lies in one of the most rocky and precipitous portions of the Epistle to the Romans, like a tiny lakelet on the bosom of gaunt and rugged cliffs: "For if by one man's offence death reigned by one, much more they which receive the abundance of grace and of the gift of righteousness shall reign in life by one, Jesus Christ" (5:17).

In those words three things are patent:

1. THE DIFFERENCES WHICH ARE PREVALENT AMONG CHRISTIANS. Some *exist;* others *live;* others again *reign in life.* Some have life, others have it "more abundantly." With some the spark of eternal life burns dimly, shrouded by dense wreaths of smoke; with others— oh that it might be with you and me, reader!—the light burns and shines clear, fervent, brilliant. To reign in life is to realize the conception of being kings and priests unto God, a royal generation, a chosen people. The conception includes nobility of demeanor, such as becomes the scion of a line of kings; munificence, as when a prince scatters his largess among the crowd; and victory, as becomes the monarch who has trod his enemies beneath his feet, climbing to his throne.

What do you know of these? Would you dare assert that there is any evidence in your days to make men think that you reign in life? Do the keys hang at your belt? Do unholy desires bite the dust in your presence? Is there nobility in your mien? Is there a consciousness among others that your religion is not only barely sufficient for your own needs, but that the grace of God has so abounded toward you that you in turn can abound to every good work? If not, you have yet to learn what it is to reign in life.

2. THE CAUSE OF THIS DIFFERENCE. It does *not* arise, thank God, from any arbitrary allotment on his part of more or less grace. "There are diversities of gifts";

but his *grace* is like the wild flowers on the common, or the beauty that lies as a bloom upon nature, or the water which he brews among the hills—all of which are free in their unrestrained abundance to every child of the family of man. Not only so, but for each one of us there is an *abundance* of grace within our reach. God is very frugal; there is no waste in creation. What seems superfluous in one direction is eagerly wrought up into fresh and necessary fabrics by armies of mysterious and insignificant workers. But just because of this, he is able to give abundantly, beyond all we ask or think, without stint; so that all are fed, and baskets are filled to the very utmost of their content. In grace, as in nature, there is a divine prodigality, beside a divine frugality. God makes all grace abound toward us. His love passes knowledge; his joy is unspeakable; his peace outstrips our understanding; his thoughts we cannot attain unto.

The real reason, then, that so many fail to reign in life is to be sought, not in some arbitrary enactment on the part of God, but in the differing powers of receptiveness which exist among his children. Some fail to receive, either because they have not learned the art, or because they have not reached that position in Christian experience in which they can avail themselves of it. See where the apostle lays the emphasis: it is they that *receive* the abundance of grace who reign. The difference therefore is not to be found on the divine side, but on the human; not in the reservoir where the gas is stored, but in the pipe where water stops the free flow to the jet.

Great saints are simply great receivers. They may be deficient in culture, education, and a thousand things which belong to others; but they have learned the happy art, denoted by that word *receive*, which is found in every part of the New Testament, and especially in connection with the Holy Spirit, which they who believe on Christ were to receive. We can never forget that he himself constantly connected that word with the Holy Spirit; as when he breathed on his disciples and said, "Receive ye the Holy Ghost!"

Do you want that royalty of manner? *Receive* it. Do you want that generosity? You have only to *receive* it. Do you want that victory? There is no other course than to *receive* it. In a word, do you want to reign in life? Then you must *receive* the abundance of grace; and the more you receive of it, the more royal will life become. What though the hill country be filled with woods, and the lowlands infested by Canaanites!—if you will receive and use the power within your reach, "no weapon that is formed against you shall prosper; and every tongue that shall rise against you in judgment you shall condemn."

3. HOW TO ACQUIRE THIS SACRED ART. It is distinct from praying. Not, indeed, that prayer does not enter into it; but that it is only the foundation from which the soul arises into the secret of receiving. None can claim but those who pray; but many pray who do not go further to receive. "Ask and receive," said our Lord, otherwise your joy will not be full. The lack of joy in Christian hearts may often be traced to a failure to discern the difference between the prayer which is only supplication and that which takes its reward from the outstretched hand of Jesus. Too often our prayers seem like lost vessels; when, in point of fact, they have come to the quays richly freighted, but we have not been there to claim our own.

Perhaps these rules may assist you to acquire this blessed art:

(A) Be sure that what you ask is according to the mind of God, offered in some promise or precept of Holy Scripture.

(B) Ask for it simply and reverently. Use the name of Jesus; that is, stand in him, and plead for his glory.

(C) Dare to believe that God does hear and answer your prayer altogether apart from the flow of emotion or the rapture of conscious possession.

(D) Go your way and reckon that God is faithful. Count on him as bound to keep his troth.

(E) Act as you would if you had all the consciousness and enjoyment possible.

Thus you will find inevitably that the mountain shall become a plain; the woods shall fade into pasture-lands; the Canaanites shall be driven before you, as the chaff of the threshing-floor before the autumn wind; and nothing shall be impossible.

19

THE CONCLUSION OF THE TASK

(JOSHUA 18–21)

> "All which is real now remaineth,
>   And faileth never;
> The hand which upholds it now, sustaineth
>   The soul forever."
> WHITTIER

THE two great tribes were thus at last settled—Judah, as Dean Stanley suggests, like a lion to guard the south, and couch in the fastness of Zion; while Ephraim, like the more peaceful but not less powerful bullock, was to rove the rich vales of central Palestine, and defend the frontier of the north. And Joshua was able to turn his attention to the several items which claim a passing notice.

1. JOSHUA ERECTED THE TABERNACLE IN SHILOH. During the march through the wilderness, when the camp was pitched, the Tabernacle occupied the center; around it were grouped the tents of the priests and Levites, while the tribes occupied specified places, three to each quarter of the compass. An attentive comparison of those positions with the territories allocated to them in the Land of Promise will reveal a striking similarity. It was as though the encampment were, in its main features,

repeated in their final settlement in the land. And to complete the parallel, the Tabernacle was now removed from Gilgal and pitched in Shiloh, which lay as nearly as possible at the heart of Canaan.

No striking landmarks distinguish this ancient site. And, unlike most of the holy places of the world, it is said to be almost entirely featureless. Imagine a somewhat wide plain, surrounded by low hills, with a rocky platform toward its northern end. This was the chosen site of the Tabernacle, after its long wanderings, erected probably on that slight plateau. And so was fulfilled the command of the great lawgiver: "It shall come to pass that the place which the Lord your God shall choose to cause his name to dwell there, thither shall ye bring all that I command you."

Here, then, in the center of the land, embosomed in the keeping of the strongest tribes, on the east side of the highway that led from Bethel to Shechem, was the chosen spot where the Tabernacle of God was among men; and he dwelt with them. Oh that they had acted as his people; then would he have wiped away every tear from their eyes! They would have overcome, and have inherited all things.

The sacred name Shiloh, which means *peace* or *rest,* was also given by the dying patriarch to the Messiah. Jesus is the center of his people. Around him they gather. Not his professing Church, not a synod or a convocation, not a creed or a ritual—but the Rest-giver himself is the center around whom the people gather. He is both head and heart, which make the body one. Life in "the heavenlies" must have its center in the risen Saviour; and just in proportion as we focus on him shall we find ourselves brought into loving fellowship with all who love him. The altar of Ed (Josh. 22:34), which was afterward reared to attest and cement the unity of Israel, was a poor device, which would not have been needed if the people had observed the practice of thrice a year gathering at God's center, Shiloh.

2. JOSHUA REBUKED THE INERTNESS OF THE PEOPLE. And Joshua said unto the children of Israel, "How long are ye slack to go in to possess the land, which the Lord God of your fathers hath given you?" (18:3). Forthwith the twenty-one commissioners arose to walk through the land, surveying it. They embodied the results in a book, in which the land was described by cities in seven portions. This they brought to Joshua. It may be that the account of what they had seen was the means under God of arousing the people from the apathy into which they had sunk.

In our own time the Spirit of God has been sending out many commissioners to pass through and describe the good land into which the heavenly Joshua would gladly lead his people. A good many books have resulted from their investigations, which have mightily stirred the hearts of God's people, so that in great numbers they have gone up to possess. And we sincerely hope that even these words may incite Christian hearts that they may be no longer slack to go in to possess the land which the God of our fathers has given us in Jesus.

There is the portion of Benjamin, the beloved of the Lord, to dwell in safety by him, covered all the day long and borne between his shoulders—the place where Eastern mothers cradle their babes, giving them warmth and easy carriage. There is the portion of Zebulun, to whose shores the illimitable ocean washes the treasures of the deep; in whose heart Gennesaret lies, with its fragrant memories of God manifest in the flesh. There is the portion of Issachar which derived treasures from the sands, emblems of the precious stones, the pearls and crystals of spiritual character. There is the portion of Asher, the oil of whose winepresses bespeaks the unction of the Holy Spirit; the strength of whose shoes betokens that invincible might which treads down serpent and scorpion. There is the portion of Naphtali, satisfied with favor, and full of the blessing of the Lord; owning rich forests, the circle of Galilee, and the garden of Palestine. Each of these is significant of spiritual endowment, which we ought to arise to possess.

Too long have we been slack to go in to possess that fullness of the Holy Spirit which might be in us as a living spring, making us perfectly satisfied; like the fountain in the courtyard of a beleaguered castle which enables the garrison to defy the siege. There is a knowledge of Jesus, a participation in his victory, a realization of blessedness, which are as much beyond the ordinary experience of Christians as Canaan was better than the wilderness. But of all this we, alas, know so little!

The causes of this inertness are many. We shrink from spiritual attainment, because it entails self-denial, the sacrifice of darling but questionable things, together with the ascent of heights where the air is rare, and the muscles become strained, and the head swims. Our love of ease, our attachment to the world, our dread of being singular, our consciousness that we should have to forego much that we cherish, if we essayed to hold fellowship with the Holy God—all these things prevail over us as the bird lime which detains the fluttering tenants of the air from their native element.

But how much we miss! The nomad life, with its frail tents, could not afford those seven tribes of Israel so much lasting enjoyment as their own freehold in Canaan. What were the pasture lands of the desert as compared to the oliveyards and vineyards of Esdraelon or Galilee? But the comparison is utterly inadequate to portray the loss to which we subject ourselves in refusing to appropriate and enjoy the blessedness which is laid up for us in Jesus. The yielded life; the members presented to Christ for his use, and held at his disposal; the cleansed heart; the victory over sin; the singleness of purpose; the unbroken fellowship; the Pentecostal fullness! Let us come to our Joshua at Shiloh, and ask him to lead us into each of these.

3. JOSHUA RECEIVED HIS OWN INHERITANCE. "The children of Israel gave him the city that he asked, even Timnath-serah, in the hill country of Ephraim" (19:50, R.V.). In the following book it is spoken of as Timnath-heres (Judges 2:9). It was "the portion of the sun."

The old veteran had deserved well of his people, and must have been glad to retire to his estate, on which the remaining twenty years of his life were spent. And the greatness of his influence may be inferred by considering the evils that overwhelmed Israel when he was taken— as the sea rushes in when the sea wall is down. His very presence among the people was a restraint. As for him and his house, he served the Lord, and maintained the sacred rites which Moses had enjoined; so that his example shone like a beacon light and kept the darkness at bay. What a significant testimony to his consistency and steadfastness is furnished by the record, "The people served the Lord all the days of Joshua." He was like the central pillar which supports the entire weight of the roof of some chapter house, with its Gothic roof, and its exquisite foliage of carved stone.

There is fascination in the name of his inheritance. The portion of the sun! Did it lie specially open toward the sun, catching the first glimpse of sunrise, and holding the last fading gleam of sunset? Perhaps so. But there seems a special beauty in the name when we associate it with his previous career of unswerving fidelity to the will of God. Like Caleb, he had wholly followed the Lord. And as the course of the one ended in fellowship, the course of the other ended in that dwelling in the Light which is the highest bliss within man's reach.

Be wholly given to God, then you too shall live in the light, as he is in the Light. The warmth of his love shall fill your emotions with its glow, and teach you the art of love; the light of his truth shall banish obscurity and ignorance from your mind, and endow it with direct and certain knowledge; the ray of his presence shall inspire you with strength, vigor, elasticity, immortal youth. Where sunshine is, there is life, health, gladness, vigorous strength.

4. JOSHUA ALSO MADE PROVISION FOR THE MANSLAYER. Six cities were apportioned, three on each side of the Jordan, central to the adjacent districts, and easily accessible. Thither the manslayer who had killed any person unwittingly and unawares might flee from the pursuit of the next of kin. The roads were kept in good repair; clearly written directions at the cross-ways indicated the route; and, according to Jewish tradition, runners, learned in the law, were stationed at various stages to direct and help the fugitive.

Once at the city walls, all breathless from his flight, the manslayer waited at the entrance of the city gate till he had stated his case to the elders, who had the right of admitting him provisionally into the city. On the appearance of the avenger of blood, the cause seems to have been finally adjudicated; and if it were clearly shown before the assembled people that there was no animosity in the blow which caused death, the manslayer was permitted to remain there, until the death of the high priest then in office.

It is interesting to note this provision, made in the Land of Promise, for the passing over of sins which were not sins of presumption. For the latter no provision was made. But, for wrongs which did not emanate from a fixed or rooted malice, there was, as in the case of sacrifices for sins of ignorance under the Levitical code, this merciful provision. Take heart, O Christian soul! You have done many evil things, in your ignorance or thoughtlessness, for which you are justly guilty, and which might well exclude you from the Land of Promise; yet, there is forgiveness for you. Only flee to the City of Refuge, which is also the city of the priests, and hide yourself there; you will not only be safe, but shall enjoy your inheritance beside, for the High Priest has died, and in his death has put away your sin forever. There is therefore now no condemnation for you, because you are in him.

The Jews particularly have acted the part of the manslayer. They killed the Prince of Life, but they did it in ignorance (Acts 3:17–18). Therefore they have lost their heritage; but they exist still as prisoners of hope, finding refuge among the cities of the priests, until such time as the Lord Jesus shall wrap up the present age as a worn-out vesture, and shall inaugurate that new and glorious reign in which he shall take to himself the kingdom. Then Israel shall return, each to his own house, and unto the city from whence he fled.

5. JOSHUA APPORTIONED CITIES FOR THE LEVITES. There was an ancient curse hanging over the lots of Simeon and Levi. Brothers by birth, they had been joint perpetrators in a dark crime which had made Jacob, their father, to stink among the inhabitants of the land, among the Canaanites and Perizzites. The dying patriarch could not forget that deed of treacherous cruelty, and as it rose before his filming sight he said:

> "Weapons of violence are their swords,
> Cursed be their anger, for it was fierce;
> And their wrath, for it was cruel;
> I will divide them in Jacob,
> And scatter them in Israel."

But this curse was not fulfilled in each case in the same way. With Simeon, it ran its course. Settled at the south of Canaan, between Judah and Philistia, this tribe became more and more nomadic, and finally faded out of corporate existence. In the case of Levi, it was transformed into blessing. The behavior of this tribe was very remarkable. At Sinai, when Moses called on all who were loyal to Jehovah to gather in the gate of the camp, the Levites, to a man, answered his appeal. Phinehas, also, who took such decisive action in the matter of Baal-peor, was a Levite—perhaps even a typical one. Whereupon Jehovah entered into a covenant of life and peace with them, took them as a substitute for the first-born sons of Israel, and pledged himself to be their inheritance (Num. 18:20; Josh. 13:33).

At the divine command, forty-eight cities were given to the Levites, with one thousand cubits of pasture land, measured outward from the city walls. There they dwelt when not required for temple service, or when they were incapacitated by age from attending on their sacred office.

As Jacob predicted, they were scattered; but the effect was most salutary. They permeated the whole land with the hallowing influence of Shiloh. What a halo of sacred interest must have gathered round the man whose lot it was to enter into the Temple of God and burn incense at the solemn hour of prayer! Then multiply this a thousandfold, and consider what a wide and wholesome effect must have been produced throughout the country, especially when Levi fulfilled the lofty possibilities of its high calling.

Moreover, the teaching of the law was a special prerogative of the Levites, who appear to have traveled through their apportioned districts. They taught Jacob God's judgments, and Israel his law; as well as put incense and whole burnt offering on the altar. They caused the people to discern between the unclean and the clean, and in a controversy stood to judge. They acted as the messengers of the Lord of Hosts (Deut. 33:10).

So the work was finished. "There failed not aught of any good thing which the Lord had spoken unto the house of Israel; all came to pass" (Josh. 21:43–45). And this is true still. Our Father has blessed us with all spiritual blessings in Christ. He has withheld no good thing. In Jesus all fullness dwells—all that is needed for life and godliness. We are complete in him. If there is failure, it is ours, not his. If the Book of Judges succeeds to that of Joshua, it is because God's heirs yield to unbelief and sin.

In the eternity, which is at hand, as we stand together and review our life course—with its battles and marches and experience, its losses and gains, its heights of privilege and depths of failure—we shall without doubt take up and repeat the glad confession of these noble words, and confess that no good thing failed us of aught that the Lord had spoken, but that all came to pass.

20

LIFE IN THE LAND

(JOSHUA 22)

"Give us now, now!—to live in the life of God.
Give us now, now!—to be at one with him."
JEAN INGELOW

W HEN the seven years of fighting came at last to an end, the children of Israel settled down to the enjoyment of their land. It was like the clear shining of the sun after a wild morning, or like a happy and prosperous manhood after a tempestuous youth. The comparative silence of the record suggests the engrossing interest with which the people gave themselves to the culture of the land, and to the occupation of great and goodly cities which they had not built, of houses full of all good things which they had not filled. Cisterns which they had not hewn poured forth refreshing waters to vineyard, oliveyard, or garden; and they ate and were full.

The soul, as it matures in Christian experience, though it never ceases to walk carefully, yet comes to realize more fully the blessings of the heavenly places. It is satisfied with the goodness of the Lord, and is like a watered garden. It is fanned by breezes from the mountains of myrrh. The air is heavy with perfume; the vines bud, their blossoms are open, the pomegranates flower, and at the door all manner of precious fruits, new and old, are laid up.

It is in such seasons that we learn the meaning of rest, find the true source of unity, and see the need of patience in dealing with the erring or fallen.

1. OUR FIRST DISCOVERY IS THE MEANING OF REST. "The Lord gave them rest round about, according to all that he sware unto their fathers" (21:44). "And now," said Joshua, addressing the two and a half tribes, "the Lord your God hath given rest unto your brethren, as he promised them." And this was the climax of Jehovah's dealings with the chosen people. For this he brought them up out of the sea with the shepherds of his flock. For this he put his Holy Spirit in the midst of them. For this he caused his right hand to go at the right hand of Moses, dividing the water before them, to make himself an everlasting name. For this he led them through the depths, as a horse in the wilderness, that they should not stumble. The divine intention through it all was that as cattle go down into the valley, with its shade and succulent pasture, to hide themselves from the burning heat, so the Spirit of the Lord should cause them to rest (Isa. 63:14).

There was a very distinct measure of rest. The land rested (Josh. 11:23), and the people also. But it is equally clear that Canaan did not exhaust God's ideal. Fair as it was, its benediction did not go beyond the narrow circle of mere worldly prosperity and material interests. And these were manifestly inadequate. How impossible it is for the soul to take its ease just because of some large increase in worldly prosperity! As well expect it to grow fat on husks! It was equally impossible that the mere possession of the Land of Promise could give rest to hearts with infinite capacity for love, or to minds with an insatiable appetite for truth. The rest of Canaan, like so much else in this book, could at best be only a type and shadow of that spiritual repose, that holy tranquility, that unspeakable peace which fills the souls of men with the rest of God himself. Listen to these words—*my* rest, *his* rest; *the Sabbath-keeping* of the people of God. These are more than Canaan, with its joys of harvest and the song of the treader in the press. Therefore, it is truly said in the Epistle to the Hebrews, "If Joshua had given them rest, he [the Spirit of inspiration by the mouth of David] would not have spoken afterward of another day. There remaineth therefore a sabbath rest for the people of God" (Heb. 4:8–9, R.V.).

There is rest from the first glad outburst of the new life; but it gets more intense as the years go on, as the hue of the sky deepens from the pale blue of April into the ultramarine of August. The cause of this is in the ever-growing conviction that God's way is perfect, his will loveliest, his plan best. When first we enter into rest, we have to watch against distrust, to reason with ourselves that all must be well, to solace ourselves with promise and assurance. But, as the days pass, each utters speech to the next; and the accumulated voice of experience gathers volume within the secret chambers of the heart. We come to *know* him whom once we did but *trust*. We remember that not one good thing has failed of all he promised. We see that the most threatening tempest clouds of our lives have either been dissipated or have broken in showers of blessing. We remember that things we prayed against, and fought against, have been our greatest blessings. We are driven to admit that whenever we got our way, it was gall and bitterness; but, when God had his, it was milk and honey.

When such thoughts throng the heart, while from some summit in life we review the past, our hearts are filled with emotions of tranquil restfulness. Why should we fret and chafe, or beat our breasts against the bars, or allow our souls to be disquieted within us? All is under law, all under love, all things are working together for good. He will give grace and glory. No good thing will he withhold from those to whom he has given his only-begotten Son. In him the tenderness of motherhood and of fatherhood blend. There is not a step he does not weigh; not a path he does not winnow; not a tear, the shedding of which has not been to him a subject of anxiety; not a stab of pain, the edge of which he has not felt before it touches us; not a sorrow, the weight of which he has not felt before he allowed it to impinge. Such a God is yours, O my soul! Hush, and trust him; he is doing all things well. Be still and at rest! You are as safe as if the gate of pearl were behind you; your joy cannot rust or be stolen. Every wind is a south wind; every shore your native land; every circumstance a rough packing case containing the gifts of your Father's love.

And so the rest, born of trust, gets ever deeper; because the trust enlarges with growing knowledge. The more we grow in the knowledge of God, and of his Son Jesus Christ, the more absolute is our trust in his everlasting, all-pervading love; and the more unbroken is our rest. It is true that the people entered into rest when they crossed the Jordan; it is also true that seven years later they drank higher up the stream, where the waters were more pellucid. This is a fitting emblem of the successive increments of restfulness experienced by those whom the Lamb leads ever farther into the heart of the land, unswept by tempests, and within the limits of which there is no more sea.

2. OUR SECOND DISCOVERY IS THE TRUE CENTER OF UNITY. The forty thousand warriors who had so nobly fulfilled their early promise received the public thanks of the great leader; and his last advice, "Turn ye, and get you unto your tents; . . . only take diligent heed to do the commandment of the Lord." He expressed also in the name of the congregation his fervent desire that they should have much cattle, silver, gold, brass, and iron, with very much raiment—words and wishes which

they most certainly deserved.

When they reached the fords of Jordan, and reflected that the stream would presently divide them from the rest of the people, a sudden fear seems to have overtaken them, lest, in coming days, the ten-and-a-half tribes might say to their children, "What have ye to do with Jehovah, the God of Israel? For the Lord hath made Jordan a border between us and you: ye have no portion with us." To obviate this, and to make clear for all coming time their identity with the rest of the people, they built an altar on the western bank of Jordan. It was a great altar to look at, not intended for burnt-offering or meal-offering or any religious rites, but as a perpetual witness that its builders were true-hearted Israelites.

But it was a great mistake. No pattern for its shape had been received from God, nor any direction as to its construction; if they only obeyed the divine instruction—that three times in the year all their males should appear before God in Shiloh—there would be no need for this clumsy contrivance. In their view the unity of the people could not be preserved by a merely spiritual bond, but needed an outward and mechanical one. The common ties of the altar at Shiloh were insufficient; there must be in addition the great altar of Ed.

There was in general understanding, however, a truer conception—that of Joshua and the rest of Israel. Similarly, life in the heavenlies begets in us a clear conception of the true unity of the people of God. And here is another remarkable parallel between this book and the Epistle to the Ephesians, which, while it is specially the book of the heavenly places, is also the revelation of the mystery of that body which, amid the diversity of its parts, partakes of the unity of God himself. In the early stages of Christian life, we suppose that unity can only be obtained by the formulation of a common creed, and the inclusion of all believers in some great visible body. We build the altar of Ed; ignorant of God's principle of unity, we make one for ourselves. In a word, we mistake *uniformity* for *unity*. But as we go from strength to strength we discover that all true souls who meet around the altar are one. Coming from all points of the compass, fired by the same hopes, suppliants at the same meeting place, reliant upon the same blood, the common attraction establishes an organic unity—like that of the tree, the multiplicity of whose parts is subsidiary to the one life force; or like that of the body, the variety of whose members is subordinate to the one animating soul.

The nearer we get to Christ, the more clearly we discern our unity with all who belong to him. We learn to think less of points of divergence and more of those of agreement. We find that the idiosyncrasies by which each believer is fitted for his specific work do not materially affect those depths of the inner life which in all saints abut on the nature of the living Saviour. As the scattered sheep browse their way up toward a common summit, they converge on each other, and there is one flock, as there is one Shepherd.

It is the supreme vision of the Bible, granted to the most eminent saints, that though the new Jerusalem comprehends the names of the tribes of Israel and of the Apostles of the Lamb, is garnished by jewels of many hues, and has gates facing in all directions, it yet is one, "the Bride, the Lamb's wife." What wonder, then, that the world, and sometimes the professing Church, supposes that the Lord's prayer is not fulfilled, and that the unity has yet to be made? The unity is made; but only the spiritual with spiritual discernment can detect its symmetry.

3. WE DISCOVER THE NEED OF PATIENCE IN DEALING WITH THE ERRING AND FALLEN. When first the tribes of Israel heard of the erection of the altar, their impulse was to go at once against their brethren to battle. Shiloh was the mustering place; for it seemed as if an offence had been perpetrated against that holy

shrine.

But wiser counsels prevailed, and it seemed best to depute Phinehas and ten princes, men of note, to go as a deputation in the name of the whole congregation of the Lord. They found the warriors in the land of Gilead on the point of dispersing to their homes, uttered their remonstrance, and quoted the warning instances of Achan and Beth-peor as reasons for fear lest the sin of one should be visited in judgment upon all. Their contention was that none of the tribes of Israel, or even of individual members of the commonwealth, could sin without involving the whole in judgment. "Rebel not against the Lord, nor rebel against us."

So deeply had the spirit of love wrought in their hearts that they even proposed to share the land of western Canaan, wherein the Lord's Tabernacle dwelt, with their brethren: "If the land of your possession be unclean, then pass ye over unto the land of the possession of the Lord, and take possession among us."

There was a gentleness, a winsomeness, a desire to attract back the erring, which are quite beautiful, and in striking contrast to much that had been, and was yet to be. And it had its desired effect in eliciting a frank disavowal of any desire to turn away from following the Lord, accompanied by a simple explanation of the motives which had actuated them. Thus the whole episode resulted in a tightening of the bonds of brotherhood, and in glad protestations of thankfulness and praise.

So is it always. The fiery persecutor ends by beseeching men by the mercies of God. The sword is laid aside for the olive branch. And we who had commenced life full of harsh judgments and impetuous heat, while not relaxing our steadfast allegiance to truth, learn to deal gently with the erring—restoring them in a spirit of meekness, bearing one another's burdens, and counting it a greater gain to win a brother than to overcome him in argument or destroy him by sarcasm. Thus, in the golden autumn, the fruit which had been acrid enough in its first inception becomes mellow and luscious. The fierce beams that struck like swords fall slanting in softening radiance; and Peter, the vehement disciple, administers consolation to suffering believers out of a heart softened by years of tempering trial.

21

TAKE HEED TO LOVE!

(JOSHUA 23)

"With all thy hart, with all thy soull and mind
Thou must him love, and his behests embrace; . . .
And give thyselfe unto him—full and free,
That full and freely gave himselfe to thee!"
SPENSER

EIGHTEEN years had probably passed since the events recorded in the previous chapter. The rest which God had given had not been broken in upon by any uprising of the Canaanites; and the people had been able to prosecute the toils of husbandry unhindered by the alarm of war. All around them, and mingled with them, were the remnants of the Canaanites; but they were becoming more accustomed to the joint occupancy of the land with the invaders, and were content to share with them a country so rich that it was easily able to sustain them all.

Meanwhile, years as they passed left evident traces on the bearing and energy of the great leader, who had become "old, and well stricken in years." In this respect, of course, he presents no parallel with the Prince and Captain of the Church, who is leading his people into the heavenly places, and sharing with them his rest. He "ever liveth." Joshua, knowing that his end was drawing near, called for the leaders of the people to an audience with him, in some such way as the great Apostle of the Gentiles summoned the elders of Ephesus to meet him on the shore of the Ægean. It must have been an imposing and memorable gathering, either in the vicinity of his own inheritance, or on the sacred site of Shiloh.

Probably Caleb would be there with Kenaz; Phinehas the priest; warriors who had been in all the great battles of the conquest, but who had latterly exchanged the sword for the plowshare, and the spear for the pruning-hook; others also who were beardless youths at the conquest, but now came as heads of families, elders, judges, and officers. The wisdom and chivalry of Israel were convoked to hear the last words of the great chief, who bridged the gulf of time between the passage of the Red Sea and that moment when the Land of Promise had been for twenty years in the possession of the people.

Standing upon the vantage ground of that gathering, Joshua directed the mind of his hearers into the past, and reminded them of what God had done for them. He had brought them in and planted them in the mountain of his inheritance, in the place which he had made for himself to dwell in; and not one thing had failed of all the good things that he had spoken; all had come to pass. This episode of the old veteran testifying to the unfailing faithfulness of God has its counterpart in the experience of the matured believer, when memory speaks, recalling scenes from the long past and comparing the harvest of life's golden autumn with the promise of its spring.

Joshua's one anxiety appears to have been about the nations that were left. Seven times he refers to the nations of the land. What God had done to them; how they were allotted to be an inheritance; how God was prepared to thrust them out; and especially how great a temptation would be suggested by their perpetual presence, lest the people should be tempted to cleave unto them, intermarry with them, and adopt their gods. It was as though the old man realized that he was the only barrier between Israel and the inroads of worldly conformity and idolatrous rites; and his exhortation anticipates that addressed by the Apostle Paul to the elders of the church at Ephesus: "I know that after my departing grievous wolves shall enter in among you, not sparing the flock, and from among your own selves shall men arise, speaking perverse things; wherefore watch ye!"

As a preservative against these evil consequences, Joshua proposed three safeguards: the *first* reminds us of the admonition given to himself at the beginning of this book, that they were to be very courageous, so as to keep and do all that was written in the law of Moses, not turning aside from it to the right hand or to the left. The *second* was the certainty that if they became identified with the heathen in marriage alliance or idolatrous practices, they would not be able to prevail against them in battle, but would find in them a trap, a scourge and thorns, until they perished quickly from off the good land into which they had come.

But it is on the *third* that we would dwell particularly: "Take good heed therefore unto yourselves, that ye love the Lord your God." There is a beautiful fitness in this exhortation as coming at the close of this book. The earlier pages are full of bloodshed and strife; but here the soldier speaks as the lover, and the clash of arms is exchanged for the dulcet notes of the harp. The froth is left behind, and the stream runs clear. The storm of the morning has sunk into the gentle zephyr of the evening sunset. Thus the life of Christ led up to the discourses of the upper room, warm with the glow of love.

The whole law of God and of human life is fulfilled in that one word, "Thou shalt love." Take good heed to love God, and all other injunctions are comparatively needless. Love God, and you will be content with nothing less than to inherit all the land, even to that great sea of his love upon which the sun never goes down. Love God, and courage must possess you; as the timid bird will assail the dreaded depredator of her nest, her maternal love making her oblivious to all considerations of her own safety. Love God, and you will love his Book, nor wish to swerve from it. Love God, and you will not seek a love which is inconsistent with your supreme affection. Love God, and you will possess God, and be possessed by God; and things which otherwise had been snares and traps and scourges will become stepping-stones to a fuller, richer life. Love God, and you will become one with all holy beings in heaven and upon earth, and throughout the universe, to whom he is the supreme Love.

The one consideration, therefore, which demands our thought is how to fulfill this command, "Take heed to love." What are the steps by which we may enter into the heart of obedience to that great law, first enunciated by Moses, and reaffirmed by Jesus, "Thou shalt love the Lord thy God with all thy heart, and with all thy soul, and with all thy mind, and with all thy strength"?

1. REMEMBER THAT LOVE IS OF GOD. The only Being that really is, is God. All other being is derived; his is inherent and essential to himself. There is probably a deeper meaning than we have ever apprehended in his name, I AM. There is one God, the Father, of whom are all things. He is over all, and through all, and in all. Therefore, all love and power and wisdom not only reside in him, but pass from him into all other beings, according to the measure in which they are prepared to receive them. He is the central Sun; and all that is fair or noble or helpful in any one is the far-traveled ray of his nature caught by the soul, consciously or not, to be flashed back again to its source.

What was nature in its first creation but the reproduction in material forms of thoughts and conceptions that otherwise had been hidden forever in the depths of the divine nature! What are the forces in the physical world—light, heat, electricity—but manifestations of the energy of God! And what, in the moral world, are virtue, courage, patience, love but sparks—more or less dimmed by the fallen state of man—of that light which lighteth every man coming into the world!

Let us ascend farther, into the highest sphere of all, and speak of love. Love is the crown of human nature; its regal chaplet of flowers; the bond by which the sentient universe is made one; the trait in which we most nearly resemble God, for God is Love. In Love's hand lies the key to unlock the lost secret of concord. She alone can speak the magic word by which the marring effect of sin can be undone, and all the occupants of the many mansions of the Father's house formed into one great family, bound together and to God by the cohesion of a common tie. It is by love alone that angels, and redeemed spirits, and holy beings everywhere shall be so harmonized as to unite in the new song, which is yet to break in waves of melody around the throne of the Most High. Love must conquer discord, subdue strife, and complete the divine purpose.

But all love—whether in the heart of the babe, that stretches out its hands toward the familiar face which overbends it; or in the mother, enthralled to a new ecstasy; or in the faithful servant, prepared to give his life for his charge; whether in the soul of man or of angel; whether on earth, or beyond it in the blessed spheres that elude our vision—must have its ultimate source, fountain, and origin in the heart of God.

It stands, therefore, to reason that those who would love purely, unselfishly, strongly, must converse deeply with God. There must be a steeping of the nature in his fellowship, as the dyer's hand in the deep colors of his craft, or sea-flowers in the warm waters of southern climes. As the moon must hold converse with the sun, that she may receive the glory which she shall transmit to our night, so our only hope of giving love is to receive it. We must get, if we would give; absorb, if we would transmit; obtain, if we would scatter. Oh for a closer walk with God!

2. BUT SUCH LOVE COMES TO US THROUGH JESUS. There is, of course, a broad sense in which the love of God reaches all men; but even this is only possible because of the death and intercession of the Lord Jesus. Unless he had become the propitiation for the sins of the world, the love of God would have had no channel through which, consistent with righteousness, it could have poured forth its tides. Had it not been for Jesus, the flowers of heaven falling into the pit of sin would have been turned to flakes of fire.

But, in a deeper sense, the love of God has been stored in the manhood of Jesus. The divine essence expresses itself in terms of human affection. And it is when we know Jesus, and are united to him by faith, and through him are united to God, that we begin to experience the full tide of divine love as it comes from God the Father, through the Son, to become in us a well of living water, springing up into everlasting life. Then we begin to experience what Paul meant when he cried, "The love of Christ constraineth us." Open your heart to Jesus; cultivate his friendship; live in his fellowship; familiarize yourself with the constant consideration of what he has done for you. Love begets love; think, then, how much he loved you, when he gave himself for you. Talk of him to others, till your soul begins to glow.

3. LOVE ALSO IS BY THE HOLY SPIRIT. The love of God has been shed abroad in our hearts by the Holy Spirit, which is given unto us (Rom. 5:5). As the grapes of Eshcol were a pledge that God would give the land from which they came, and he did, so the divine Spirit takes of the love of Christ, and communicates it to us, as an assurance of a hope that can never be ashamed. We argue from the bliss which is to that which is to be. We are

sure of eternity because it is already begun in us. Already we hunger no more, neither thirst any more; and are therefore assured of the land where the Lamb leads his flock to fountains of life.

Let us lay this well to heart, that the first fruit of the Spirit is love. Like fruit, it swells gradually on the bough, reddens in the cluster, and ripens, man hardly knows how. Yield to the Holy Spirit; never rest till you have claimed, reverently and humbly, your share in Pentecost; be filled with the Spirit: thus you, too, will receive a baptism of love. When we are strengthened by the Holy Spirit in the inner man, we begin to know the heights and depths, and lengths and breadths of the love of Christ.

4. THERE ARE SOME FURTHER DIRECTIONS FOR LOVING GOD. We can only enumerate them as we close:

(A) Distinguish between the emotion of love, which is variable and inconstant, and love itself.

(B) Remember that it is possible to love God not only with the heart, but with the mind. The will should put him first, as the pivot upon which the whole life shall revolve.

(C) The test of love is not feeling or speaking, but obeying. "He that hath my commandments, and keepeth them, he it is that loveth me."

(D) Guard against the intrusion of sense; for where any license is given to bodily appetite, there is instant loss inflicted on the growth of the soul in the love of God.

(E) Climb to the love of God through the love of man. Dare to treat all men as you know you would if you *felt* like loving them, and you will come to feel tenderly and pitifully toward them. This is the beginning of love. This is most like God's love. Act thus always by the power of the indwelling Spirit, and you will certainly apprehend in growing measure, though never comprehend, the unsearchable love of God. We may know the love of Christ; but it passeth knowledge.

EVENSONG

(JOSHUA 24)

"Whensoe'er it comes—
That summons that we look for—it will seem
Soon, yea, too soon!—Let us take heed in time
That God may now be glorified in us!"
H. HAMILTON KING

ONCE more the veteran leader, who was soldier, judge, statesman, and prophet combined, desired to see his people face to face. His meeting with their representatives was therefore followed, almost immediately, by a gathering of all the tribes of Israel to Shechem, where years before they had stood together in solemn convocation while from the heights of Ebal and Gerizim had rolled the Amens of the people in answer to the blessing and the curse.

The stones on which the law had been written were still clearly in evidence, and the whole scene must have come vividly back to the memory of the majority of those assembled. But from that moment the valley would be associated specially with this touching farewell scene, in which Joshua uttered his last exhortations and appeals.

JOSHUA'S NARRATIVE. He told again the wonderful story of Israel's past, beginning where God began, with their fathers in their native land beyond the Euphrates, in the dim dawn of history. What a far-traveled look was that to Terah, the father of Abraham and the father of Nachor! The reference was possibly intended to give him the opportunity of emphasizing the fact that there the family was as much addicted to idolatry as any of the peoples around. This sin was, so to speak, indigenous to the soil of Israel—a weed which would crop up, unless the utmost care was exercised against it. Look, O Israel, to the hole of the pit whence you were hewn; you were not originally one whit better than others. God did not choose you for any distinguishing trait of monotheistic fervor, but because of his sovereign grace. This alone has made you to differ. You were dead in trespasses and sins; but in his mercy, for his great love wherewith he loved you, God chose you for his own.

Isaac, Jacob, Esau—names which made the deepest chords vibrate in his hearers' hearts—were successively recalled in the deep hush that had fallen on the vast assembly. Then the speaker, acting as the spokesman of Jehovah, reached more familiar ground, as he recalled names and events which had played a part in his own wonderful career: the mission of the two brothers, Moses and Aaron; the plagues of Egypt; the cry and deliverance at the Red Sea; the wilderness; Balak, son of Zippor, and Balaam, son of Beor; the passage of the Jordan; the fall of Jericho; the overthrow of the seven nations of Canaan; the possession of their land.

But throughout the story the entire stress is laid on grace, by the God who says: I took; I gave; I sent; I brought; I destroyed; I gave; I delivered. Not a mention is made of Israel's mighty men. All is attributed to the ultimate source of nature, history, and grace—the supreme will of God. We cannot get beyond that. However many links we interpose between ourselves and the causes of things, ultimately we are shut up to acknowledge the determining counsel and foreknowledge of God.

The Christian cannot improve on the creed once formulated by the great heathen monarch Nebuchadnezzar: "He doeth according to his will in the army of heaven, and among the inhabitants of the earth; and none can stay his hand, or say unto him, What doest thou?"

There is nothing more salutary than to stand on the eminence of the years in life's golden evening and review the way by which our God has led us. The faraway home, where faces glimmer out in the daybreak of life's morning, on which we shall not look again till the vail of eternity rends; the hard bondage of early life; the many straits and deliverances; the guiding cloud of the pilgrimage; the daily provision for incessant needs; the human love; the goodness and mercy which have followed all our days. Ah me—what a romance lies behind the meanest life, of sin and forgiveness, of provocation and pity, of grace and gift! Not one of us is there that shall not hold his own history to be the most wonderful of all when we exchange experiences in that land which we shall not get by our own sword or bow, dwelling in mansions we did not build, eating of vineyards and oliveyards we did not plant.

JOSHUA'S APPEAL.   It would appear that the people largely maintained the worship of household gods, like those which Rachel stole from Laban. This practice was probably perpetuated by stealth. But the germs of evil were only awaiting favorable conditions to manifest themselves, and Joshua had every reason to dread the further development of the insidious taint. The human heart is always so willing to substitute the material for the spiritual; and where the idol takes the place of God, man forfeits the only antagonistic force strong enough to counteract the workings of his passion. Thus in every nation under heaven idolatry has sooner or later led to impurity. Therefore, with marked emphasis, Joshua appealed to the people to put away the gods which Terah and others of their ancestors had served beyond the River, and those which they had vainly invoked in the slave-huts of Egypt. He did this first at the close of his address (v. 14) and again just before the memorable interview closed (v. 23).

The work of idol-renunciation runs parallel with our deepest experiences in the blessed life. Even John, at the close of his first Epistle, bids his disciples keep themselves from idols. In fact, it is only as the clearer light of heaven falls upon us that we come to see the true nature of many things which we had counted innocent, and hugged as dearer than life. We may choose death once for all in some solemn hour of consecration, but we only gradually come to learn all that it involves. Self is our greatest idol; and it is so ubiquitous, so insidious, so protean! Scotched in one place, it breaks out in another. It clings and twines about things which are innocent enough in themselves, but which it transforms into idols, and then they have to be put away. Our Isaacs! our Rachels! our right hands!

Our only hope is to be strong in our choice of God. The negative destruction of self is unsatisfactory. We must deliberately set ourselves toward God. Our will must crown him. Our soul must make him first. Our life must be subdued to the least syllable of his command. If you would do this, peace would come to you. "If it seem evil unto you to serve the Lord, choose you this day whom ye will serve; whether the gods which your fathers served that were beyond the River, or the gods of the Amorites, in whose land ye dwell: but as for me and my house, we will serve the Lord" (v. 15, R.V.).

THE PEOPLE'S FIRST REPLY. They professed that they had no desire to forsake Jehovah and serve other gods. They freely acknowledged that they owed everything to him from the exodus to the possession of Canaan. They also expressed their determination to serve the Lord.

JOSHUA'S ANSWER. Whether they uttered all these

vows in thunderous unison, or by the mouth of chosen representatives, or whether the historian gathered up thus the consensus of their feeling as it passed from lip to lip, we cannot tell. But surely Joshua detected some traces of insincerity in their voice. Perhaps he felt the unreality of their professions because they gave no sign of abandoning their strange gods. Had he hoped for a repetition of the scene that had taken place on that very spot so many years before, when at the challenge of Jacob his household gave unto him all the strange gods which were in their hands, and the rings which were in their ears, and Jacob hid them beneath the oak which was by Shechem (Gen. 35:2–4)? Did he expect that the leaders of the people would first bring out their contributions to a pile similar to that which, in Christian centuries, rose in the great square of Florence, at the summons of Savonarola?

But there was no such response. The people contented themselves with their affirmations, but made no sacrifices. There was no holocaust, and Joshua was deeply conscious of the unreality of profession that went no deeper than words. This, said he in effect, is no way to serve the Lord. He is a holy God; he is a jealous God. He will search out these secret sins of yours; he will not be content with the service of the lip; he will not pass over transgression and sin, even though they be hidden in the recesses of your tents and the depths of your hearts. Notwithstanding all the good that he has done to you, he will not pass over the declensions and backslidings of his people.

THE PEOPLE'S SECOND REPLY. They were full of self-confidence, and vowed, come what might, that they would serve the Lord. There was the energy of their own self-will, the strength of their own resolve, the repeated insistence on their choice of Jehovah. Standing there with Joshua they forgot the many failures of the past, mocked at his fears, derided his suggestions of possible declension, and cried, "Nay, but we will serve the Lord."

What a commentary on those proud words is given by the Book of Judges! Serve the Lord! The very first sentence which follows the record of Joshua's death in that book tells us that "the children of Israel did that which was evil in the sight of the Lord, and served Baalim; and they forsook the Lord God of their fathers" (2:11-12). And this record recurs with melancholy monotony on nearly every page. We are reminded of that other scene when beneath Sinai, burning with fire, the people pledged themselves to do all that the Lord had spoken; and within six weeks were worshiping him under the form of a calf, with lascivious dance.

In point of fact, resolution, however good and however strongly expressed, is not sufficient to carry us forward into a life of obedience. Our moral nature has become so weakened by repeated failure that it is not able to resist the appeals of sense. To will is present with us, but how to perform that which is good we find not. No one can look thoughtfully into the workings of his own nature without realizing the terrible paralysis which has befallen it. The will sits amid the vassals of the inner realm, issuing commands which it is not able to enforce, like a puppet king in the midst of mighty chiefs who dispute his authority.

Thus it is that so often young hearts are embittered with disappointment, because in some high moment of resolve they determine that all life shall be new, inspired by constant resolve, and climbing with undeviating purpose the steeps of purity and devotion; but when they descend to the plain of commonplace, to the routine of daily life, they discover that the impetus has died away, and that the power to execute the high purpose of the soul is gone. No, consecration is only possible when it is conceived, prosecuted, and consummated in power not our own, and in the energy of the Holy Spirit.

JOSHUA'S SECOND ANSWER. "Ye are witnesses," he said, "against yourselves, that ye have chosen the Lord, to serve him." In other words, he appealed to them on the ground of their own asseverations, and sought to bind them to the vows they had made. Did he not intend to probe them deeper, to make them realize the solemnity of the occasion, to compel them to face the greatness of the responsibility they had assumed? By the magnitude of the interests involved, by the mercies and deliverances of God, by the memory of their ancestors, by the great days of Abraham and Isaac, by their own solemn protestations, he urged them to be true.

THE PEOPLE'S THIRD REPLY. "We are witnesses," they cried—as in after-days the people met Pilate's repeated challenge by the imprecation upon themselves of the blood of Jesus. Alas for their self-confident boast, for their headstrong pride of purpose! "By strength can no man prevail." O my soul, be warned, that when you are challenged as to your resolves, you must make your boast in God—setting up your banners in his name, entrenching yourself within the circle of his environing Almightiness. Only by your God can you leap over a wall, or run through a troop. Ask the Holy Spirit to bind you by cords to the altar of self-surrender: by the blood-red cord of Calvary; by the silver cord of hope in the Second Advent; by the golden cord of daily fellowship.

JOSHUA'S RESPONSE. Further words were fruitless, and so he set up a memorial of the pledges by which the people had bound themselves. He wrote their words in the book of the law of God; and he took a great stone, and set it up there under the oak. "Behold," said he, "this stone shalt be a witness against us; for it hath heard all the words of the Lord which He spake unto us: it shall be therefore a witness against you, lest ye deny your God" (R.V.). Then he dismissed the people to their homes.

THERE IS COMFORT SUGGESTED TO US BY CONTRAST WITH THIS SOLEMN SCENE. Even in the Land of Promise the people introduced the old Sinaitic spirit of duty and obedience as the condition of their tenure. They had said at Sinai, "All that the Lord says, we will do." And they said it again in Canaan. And we are all apt to make the same mistake. We once sought to justify ourselves by our own efforts, and now we seek to sanctify ourselves. Once we made resolutions to earn heaven by good works; now we make them to maintain our vows of consecration intact. And as soon as we attempt to tread the difficult path of sanctification in our own energy, and by our own might, we expose ourselves to endless misery and chagrin. There is no thoroughfare by this route. We cannot perfect in the flesh that which we began in the Spirit.

Joshua did not give the people rest. Had he done so, David would not have spoken of another day. Canaan was only the *type* of the Sabbath-keeping of the people of God, but did not exhaust it. At the best it was only a material and unsatisfying type. It afforded rest from the fatigues of the march, but not to the infinite capacities of the soul. The produce of wheat fields and vineyards and oliveyards could not appease the appetite for the infinite that must have made itself felt even in the heart of Israel, as the nation settled in its God-given land. Therefore, as the Holy Spirit tells us, there remained over and above a rest which is open by faith to the people of God of every age.

Notice the deep spiritual truth here. Israel could not enter on the real rest of God, because the people persisted in introducing this talk about what they would or would not do. God's rest cannot be entered thus. Though it was the leadership of Joshua, it was the spirit of Moses. And the law can in no shape or form give rest. Is not this why so many Christians miss it still? They profess to be under the captaincy of the true Joshua; but they are all the while counting on their own resolves and boasting in their own strength.

It is only when we apprehend the provisions of the

New Covenant, which does mention man, but is full of the *"I wills"* of God, that we come into the true blessedness of rest and peace. Not what you do, but what God will do; not your bow and spear, but his right hand and his holy arm; not the energy of your good self, but the freeness of his grace. Only when you confess yourself powerless to maintain the attitude of consecration and cast yourself helplessly on him to perform all things in and through you, realizing his ideals and fulfilling his purposes, and when the entire burden is relinquished and you are content to work out in the strength of his Spirit what he works in—only then will you experience the fullness of that rest which is deep as God's, like the azure sky that slumbers behind the bars of gold which encase the glory of sunset.

His task ended, Joshua retired to his inheritance; but the influence of his character and life was felt as long as he lived, and afterward. At last he died, one hundred and ten years old, and they buried him. All Israel probably gathered to pay homage to his memory. He richly merited all the honor that he received. He had none of the gifts of Moses. He may be compared to the man of two talents, while his great master was dowered with five. But he was strong and wise and true to the great trust committed to his care by the people and by God; and amid the stars that shine in the firmament of heaven, not the least bright or clear is the luster of Joshua, the son of Nun, the antitype of the risen and ascended Saviour, and whose worthiest epitaph, as written by a subsequent hand, is—

JOSHUA,

THE SON OF NUN,

THE SERVANT OF

JEHOVAH.

This book was produced by the Christian Literature Crusade. We hope it has been helpful to you in living the Christian life. CLC is a literature mission with ministry in over 45 countries worldwide. If you would like to know more about us, or are interested in opportunities to serve with a faith mission, we invite you to write to:

Christian Literature Crusade
P.O. Box 1449
Fort Washington, PA 19034